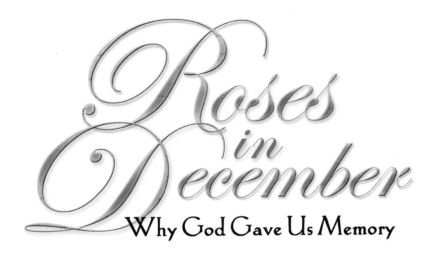

Roses in December

Why God Gave Us Memory

Jane McWhorter

D1446032

Publishing Designs, Inc.
Huntsville, Alabama

Publishing Designs, Inc.
P.O. Box 3241
Huntsville, Alabama 35810

All scripture quotations, unless otherwise indicated, are tak-
en from the New King James Version. Copyright © 1982 by
Thomas Nelson, Inc. Used by permission. All rights reserved.

Printed in the United States of America

ISBN 978-0-929540-58-0

Library of Congress Cataloging-in-Publication Data

McWhorter, Jane, 1935-
  Roses in December / Jane McWhorter.
    p. cm.
  ISBN 978-0-929540-58-0 (alk. paper)
  1. Bible—Meditations. 2. Memory—Religious aspects—Christianity. I. Title.
  BS491.5.M39 2007
  242'.5—dc22
                    2007000024

Dedication

To my loving family

*Thanks for the precious memories we have
shared during the happy times as well as the
tough ones. I love you dearly.*

The years fall gently from thee,
love . . . as petals,
when the blossom's done.
I gather each one tenderly
and save the petals,
one by one.
I place each one within
my heart and very slowly,
one by one,
the petals form a rose again . . .
forever sweet,
forever young.

Author Unknown

Contents

A Rose for Jane

As Jane has recounted the memories from years past that are now becoming *Roses in December*, she is totally unaware that she is a precious rose in so many lives. She has inspired thousands with her writings; many hundreds have been fed from her own pocketbook; and hundreds of nursing home residents have been cheered by cards, flowers, candy, and balloons when no one else, not even their own families, seemed to care. She is a pen pal to countless prisoners who are so lonely. She has graded more than five thousand Bible correspondence courses, writing personal letters with each lesson to explain answers. She always includes a paragraph praising and encouraging them in their desire to study the Word of God.

Women have learned to love and obey God through Jane's classes and one-to-one teaching. Cards and calls come in almost daily, thanking her for caring. She has received numerous letters from people who are now in their midlife years, but we knew them when they were teenagers. They still remember "little" things Jane did thirty or forty years ago that had great impact upon them. After her critical injuries in 2005 she received nearly a thousand cards from forty-four states, all of them mentioning ways she had touched their lives.

Those who benefit from Jane's lovely life are those closest to her—her own family. Her labor of love has sustained us in countless ways. Her faith has inspired us, and her courage to survive and to continue actively serving God has strengthened us. As the one who has lived with her more than fifty years, I can say with all sincerity that she is the most Christ-like person I have ever known. Such intimate knowledge is sure to reveal the whole person, thorns and all. But if there are any thorns, I have never found one.

There are many ways to preserve roses to keep them special and very precious. But the treasured roses are held dear only because they were special when they were fresh blossoms. Enjoy roses while they live and preserve their memories for December. Our children, grandchildren, and countless others will preserve Jane in memory for the years to come.

To Jane, my precious wife: I will enjoy you as a beautiful blossom my whole life. You are a rose in so many lives, but mine most of all.

—Don

Introduction

Priceless memories! It is sad, but true, that the passing of time often brings a deeper appreciation of yesterday's fleeting moments. When we are young, we usually live in the present and long for the future, with little thought of the treasures stored within our hearts.

The seeds of this study were first planted thirty year ago when my daddy brought some boxes to our house from the attic of my childhood home in Nashville, Tennessee, shortly after the death of my mother. There were scrapbooks, pictures, letters, diaries, report cards, and mementos of special events in my life. Because I had not seen most of the contents since my girlhood, opening those boxes brought floods of memories that were just as vivid as the day they happened. At that time I thought, *Someday I'm going to write a study for ladies' Bible classes on the power of memories, both good and bad.* Good intentions have a way of eluding us. We mean well, but . . .

Eighteen years later, a second incident caused me to appreciate the power of memories even more. Because my daddy was growing frail, I decided to capture the tales of his colorful childhood in his own voice on an audiotape for our grandchildren to hear in years to come. While he was visiting our home about six months before his death, he and I sat down with a recorder and just talked about what life was like in Franklin, Tennessee, during the early 1900s—playing under the house with his red fire engine, going with his father, a horse-and-buggy doctor, to make house calls, his escapades at school, his trips to Hawaii with the merchant marines, working in the orchards of California, meeting my mother, and their early years together, and the retelling of countless other stories from his life. What treasures!

When Daddy passed away just a few months after our recording session, a third incident sharpened my awareness of the power of memories. Greg, our son, brought to our house two or three boxes from the attic in my daddy's latest home. He had always been a packrat. Much of the *stuff* in the boxes should have been thrown away many years ago because it was just *junk*. However, there were some nuggets of gold in those well-worn cardboard boxes—pictures of my daddy that I had never seen; the letter his father had written to him when the rebellious teenager had left home to join the merchant marines; the words he had penned to my mother's father, asking for her hand in marriage; and many other priceless possessions. Stored in one of those boxes was one of Daddy's treasures—his little red fire engine with Franklin's dirt still clinging to its wheels.

As I sat there, surrounded by the mosaic of Daddy's life, I thought to myself, *These particles of the past should not be stuffed into boxes and stored in a musty attic. Instead, they should be passed on to the next generation as part of their own DNA of who they are and where they have come from.* That red fire engine was so symbolic of something precious to my daddy that it needed a place of honor. It found that place on a special shelf in the den, along with his worn cap pistol and special pictures.

With determination I began the task of adding our own family's memorabilia to those of my daddy's keepsakes by dragging out all of our own snapshots, school awards, letters, and other precious items from the closets, drawers, and boxes. Beginning with the year 1898—the date of a family picture made on the front porch of my great-grandfather's home—I pieced together the narrative of our family in a number of scrapbooks for each of our children, identifying the people and giving the approximate dates.

At this point, my intention for doing a study on the power of memories was still just that—a good intention. During the next few years my project fluttered in the breeze as I occasionally brainstormed some ideas on a sheet of paper in my Bible, but the project never really gained any altitude.

This book might only be a fluttering today, if it had not been for the power of a fourth incident: the fiftieth reunion of my high school class. I had not attended one in the previous forty-seven years, and it was amazing how much everyone else had changed!

Before the dinner, most of the class members were looking at one another's senior picture identification tags before initiating conversation. Once the program got underway, however, all of us were transported back to the halls of our alma mater. As antics were told, school songs were sung, and events were re-lived, we could almost feel the oiled floors beneath our feet and smell the blackboards. Even though the school building had long since been gone, our roots, our struggles, our victories, our joys, and our tears were just as fresh as if they had happened only yesterday. Oh, the transporting power of memories! I left the building that evening with a resolve to *do* something with the ideas I had carried close to my heart for so long. I began to write *Roses in December.*

Approximately two years after my high school reunion, while working on this book, an unexpected package arrived in the mail from one of my high school classmates. In cleaning out some boxes in her attic, she discovered some fifty-year-old memorabilia. She enclosed two yellowed copies of the *Litton Blast,* our high school newspaper, because it contained some articles of interest to me. She had also found her scrapbook from high school days with many clippings about school events. Unselfishly, she sent it to two classmates who host a yearly re-union at their farm near Nashville so it could be enjoyed by all. In a later letter she related how much that scrapbook had meant, especially to one of our classmates who had been diag-nosed with cancer and given only six months to live. He wrote to her, expressing his appreciation because he had kept no keepsakes of those days. He made copies for his grandchildren because he felt he could have no greater gift to pass on to them.

Roses in December is not a compilation of my remembrances. Instead, it is an in-depth study of the transforming power of memories. We will explore the importance God placed on remembering in several different categories, noting particularly the observance of the Passover in the Old Testament and the Lord's supper in the New Testament, in addition to the Jewish Feast of Purim. We will consider memory's transporting power as well as the fundamentals of how memory works and the dynamics of both short-term and long-term memory.

Not all memories are pleasant. If we are honest, we all have a few dark ones tucked deeply inside our beings. What can a Christian do to alleviate the pain of hurtful memories?

This book also carries the reader beyond the factual aspects of memory to delve into some practical ways of shaping memories for our children, other family members, and all those around us. We will share ideas on preserving our own memories. The last chapter, dealing with our memories of God, is probably the most important one of all.

Please accept my personal invitation to walk with me on this unique journey into the mirror of your life: the crucible that has greatly shaped the person you are today.

—Jane McWhorter
February 2007

Dad, Richard Shannon, with daughter Jane, 3 months

Jane at age two.

Jane, age 2, with her puppy

Jane, age 3

ARMY AIR FORCES
CHANUTE FIELD, ILLINOIS

Oct. 19, 1943
Chanute Field, I

Dear mother

RANTOUL, ILL.
OCT
930 AM
1943

M. Hicks
#1
houn City,
Miss.

Walking Down God's Memory Lane

The Bible is a treasure chest of examples of remembrances; their golden threads run throughout the pages of the Scriptures. Beginning in Genesis with God's covenant with Noah (Genesis 9:15) and continuing to the His rebuke of ungodly Babylon (Revelation 18:5), the inspired writers chronicled various nuances of the words *remember* and *memory*. Although space will not permit a detailed study of each passage, I invite you to glimpse into a few highlights.

Old Testament Examples

Noah

After 150 days of floodwater on the earth, God "remembered Noah, and every living thing, and all the animals that were with him in the ark. And God made a wind to pass over the earth, and the waters subsided" (Genesis 8:1). After Noah built an altar on the dry land, God made a covenant with this patriarch and his sons. Never again would the earth be destroyed by water. The token of that covenant was to be the rainbow. "The rainbow shall be in the cloud, and I will look on it to remember the everlasting covenant between God and every living creature of all flesh that is on the earth" (Genesis 9:16). The beautiful rainbow is God's visual reminder of His promise to Noah and his family. Each time we look at this beauty of nature, we are reminded of that promise.

Joseph

Every Bible student is familiar with the story of Joseph and his two companions in Pharaoh's prison—the chief butler and the chief baker—who had offended their ruler. Joseph interpreted a dream for each of them. The baker's dream bore ill will; three days later he was beheaded. The interpretation of the butler's dream was more favorable, however, and he was restored by Pharaoh to his former position. "Yet the chief butler did not remember Joseph, but forgot him" (Genesis 40:23).

After the passing of two years, Pharaoh himself had a perplexing dream. Its interpretation even eluded the wise men of the court. Finally the light dawned upon the chief butler as he said, "I remember my faults this day" (Genesis 41:9). He went on to tell Pharaoh about a young foreign prisoner who could interpret dreams. The rest of the story is history.

Sabbath Day

What an awesome sight Mount Sinai must have been with the quaking, thunder, lightning, and thick clouds of smoke ascending like the smoke of a furnace. Out of the midst of this spectacular sight descended the leader of the nation of Israel with two tables of stone containing the Ten Commandments. One of those commandments had its roots in the early dawn of creation: "Remember the Sabbath day, to keep it holy" (Exodus 20:8).

Jehovah then explained that this remembrance was based upon the fact that He Himself had rested on the seventh day. Each week he wanted His people to rest from their labors, just as He had done, and remember the majesty of the Creator. Remembering and resting were so important that one day each week was to be set aside for that purpose.

Exodus 31:12–17 further emphasizes the importance Jehovah placed upon the Sabbath as a means of remembering. "It is a sign between Me and the children of Israel forever; for in six days the Lord made the heavens and the earth, and on the seventh day He rested and was refreshed" (Exodus 31:17).

In the listing of the Ten Commandments in Deuteronomy, additional light is shed on the reason for resting:

> And remember that you were a slave in the land of Egypt, and the Lord your God brought you out from there by a mighty hand and by an outstretched arm; therefore the Lord your God commanded you to keep the Sabbath day (Deuteronomy 5:15).

Jehovah wanted His people to rest from their labors just as He had done.

No more would the Israelites have to work continuously in slave labor. Now each week there would be one day of rest from honest work and for remembering the mighty hand of God.

The Israelites Admonished to Remember

Moses told the people to remember their rebellion toward God from the time they left the land of Egypt until that present time (Deuteronomy 9:7–8). He elaborated on their disobedience—climaxing in the making of the golden calf—while he was on the mountain receiving the Ten Commandments. He then reminded them of their sinfulness in several other places, concluding with these words in verse 24: "You have been rebellious against the Lord from the day that I knew you." What terrible things to remember!

Moses concluded by stating that he had asked Jehovah to remember something—His promises to Abraham, Isaac, and Jacob. He had then asked God to overlook the rebellion and stubbornness of the Israelites during the wilderness years, remembering that they were His chosen people.

Milestones in Remembering Slavery

As the time drew near for the invasion and the possession of the promised land, the Israelites' doubts and fears were to be dispelled by remembering what God had done to Pharaoh and all Egypt (Deuteronomy 7:17–18).

When a good land was promised, God's people were also admonished to "remember that the Lord your God led you all the way these forty years in the wilderness, to humble you and test you, to know what was in your heart, whether you would keep His commandments or not" (Deuteronomy 8:2). Their wilderness hardships were for a purpose. They were not to forget the reason.

Wealth and the good life can cause people to forget God today just as it did thousands of years ago. In the same context, God's people were warned not to forget all He had done for them when they prospered (Deuteronomy 8:11–20).

The Jews were commanded to observe three main feasts each year to help them remember their slavery and hardships in the wilderness (Deuteronomy 16:16):

1. The Feast of Unleavened Bread (Passover)
2. The Feast of the Tabernacles (Feast of Booths)
3. The Feast of Weeks (Pentecost)

✠ *The Feast of Unleavened Bread (Passover)* will be fully discussed later. For now, we'll summarize its purpose. It was designed to commemorate the night the Lord passed over the houses of the Israelites where the blood of a lamb had been sprinkled. Inside those humble dwellings God's people had stood with staffs in hand, awaiting their deliverance as the Lord had promised. Once each year, in late March or early April, the Jews were to remember that significant night in Egypt when they were freed from slavery.

- *The Feast of the Tabernacles (Feast of Booths)* was observed at harvest time in early fall. Its purpose was twofold. Dwelling in booths made of tree branches and palm leaves for seven days was designed to help the Israelites remember their vintage life and also their years of wandering in the wilderness without any permanent dwellings.

  The advantage of remembering the days of slavery in Egypt also prompted the giving of a commandment in Deuteronomy 24:17–18. The Israelites were admonished not to take advantage of strangers, the fatherless, and widows: "But you shall remember that you were a slave in Egypt, and the Lord your God redeemed you from there; therefore I command you to do this thing." Later in that chapter the same reasoning prompted the law pertaining to leaving part of the crops in the fields and vineyards for the strangers, the fatherless, and the widows. "And you shall remember that you were a slave in the land of Egypt; therefore I command you to do this thing" (Deuteronomy 24:22).

"Remember that you were a slave in Egypt, and the Lord your God redeemed you from there."

- *The Feast of Weeks (Pentecost)* was observed in late May or early June and celebrated the close of the grain harvest. In commemoration of the time when the Israelites were homeless in Egypt, they were admonished to remember their servants, the strangers, the fatherless, and the widows among them because they themselves were once bondmen in Egypt (Deuteronomy 16:12).

God did not want His people to forget all those years of back-breaking slavery in a foreign land. That remembrance should have prompted their thankfulness for the overseeing hand of God.

Further admonitions regarding the remembrance of slavery can be found in Numbers 11:4–15. The people grew restless. Growing weary of the monotony of manna, God's people complained,

> Who will give us meat to eat? We remember the fish which we ate freely in Egypt, the cucumbers, the melons, the leeks, the onions, and the garlic; but now our whole being is dried up; there is nothing at all except this manna before our eyes! (Numbers 11:4–6).

Because the people's whining and complaining were more than Moses could bear, God told His faithful leader to select seventy men to help him in settling disputes. Later, in the same chapter, the Jews got their meat in the form of quail. After gorging themselves, many were smitten with a plague.

Fringes on Garments
God instructed Moses to command the people to make fringes on the borders of their garments

> that you may look upon it and remember all the commandments of the Lord and do them, and that you may not follow the harlotry to which your own heart and your own eyes are inclined, and that you may remember and do all My commandments, and be holy for your God (Numbers 15:38–40).

Signs on Doorposts
In an effort to help the Israelites remember some of God's most important commands, He reminded them through Moses that the divinely inspired words should be written in their own

hearts before they even tried to teach them to someone else (Deuteronomy 6:4–6).

Next, the parents were to instruct their children throughout the day's activities, beginning when they got out of bed, as they were going about household activities, when they walked outside their homes, and as they went to bed at night. In other words, faithful parents were first to remember God's inspired words themselves. Then they were to take every advantage of helping their children remember what God had said.

In addition to parents' committing God's commands to their own hearts and orally teaching them to their children throughout the day, Jehovah designed a third method. Some of these divine commands were written on parchment and then covered with leather—frontlets or phylacteries—to be worn on their heads and as well as on their arms. Those designed for the arm were usually tied on the left arm, a little below the elbow. The ones for the head were tied and worn resting on the forehead. What powerful visual aids were given to help the Israelites remember the importance of God's words!

Jehovah reminded them that the divinely inspired words should be written in their own hearts before they even tried to teach them to someone else.

Remember Miriam

Deuteronomy 24:9 urged God's people to "remember what the Lord your God did to Miriam." Numbers 12:1–16 recounts the story of the disobedience of Aaron and Miriam that was sparked by Moses' choice of an Ethiopian woman as his wife. In jealousy the two tried to undermine his authority by claiming that God had also spoken by them.

Jehovah called the three siblings to the tabernacle, where He came down in the pillar of a cloud and spoke to them, confirming His choice of Moses as His spokesman.

When the cloud departed, God's anger was manifested in Miriam's sudden leprosy. (The Scriptures do not reveal why Aaron was spared.) Because of her disobedience, the entire nation of Israel—thousands of people—stopped and waited for the allotted seven days for Miriam's purification.

The Israelites were later admonished by Moses to remember what had happened to Miriam as a reminder that disobeying God can only lead to heartaches.

Some Parting Words of Moses

Shortly before the death of Moses, he wrote what is called "The Song of Moses" (Deuteronomy 32:1–43). In verse 7 he advised them to "remember the days of old, consider the years of many generations. Ask your father, and he will show you; your elders, and they will tell you." What a heritage the Israelites had to remember—all their ancestors' blessings as well as their wrongs. Sadly, the remembering didn't always help them do what was right.

When Moses died on Mount Nebo and Joshua assumed his position of leadership, the new leader told the people to "remember the word which Moses the servant of the Lord commanded you, saying, 'The Lord your God is giving you rest and is giving you this land'" (Joshua 1:13). They needed that memory to give them courage for the task that lay ahead.

A Memorial at Gilgal

Memorials are visual reminders of significant events. In Washington, D.C., a number of structures have been erected to enable the citizens to remember the significance of some important people or events, such as the Lincoln Memorial, the Washington Monument, and the Vietnam Wall.

Jehovah wanted the Israelites to remember their miraculous crossing of the Jordan River when they entered the promised land (Joshua 4:1–24). After the people had passed over to dry ground, twelve men—a representative from each tribe—each took a stone from the river and carried it to the other side to be set up as a memorial in Gilgal.

The people were instructed to relate this awesome event when their children asked, "What are these stones?" The parents were to tell the younger ones about walking through the Jordan River on dry land, just as they had done forty years before when the Red Sea had opened up for their passage.

The twelve stones helped them remember. That was important.

All the Israelites needed to be aware of two miraculous passages through large bodies of water. They also needed to be reminded of the power of God and His providence. The twelve stones helped them remember. That was important.

Samson

When Delilah tricked Samson, a judge of Israel, into telling her the secret of his strength, the Philistines captured him, put out his eyes, and brought him bound to Gaza. At the time of sacrifice to the pagan god Dagon, the lords of the Philistines made sport of Samson by calling for him to be set between the pillars of the temple.

After asking to feel the pillars of the building, Samson called unto the Lord and said, "O Lord God, remember me, I pray! Strengthen me, I pray, just this once, O God, that I may with one blow take vengeance on the Philistines for my two eyes!" (Judges 16:28).

Because Samson's hair had grown back between the time of his capture and this event, his strength had returned. By taking hold of the two middle pillars of the temple, he was able to kill more people at the time of his death than during his lifetime.

Samson had asked the Lord to remember him. God listened.

Hannah's Request for Remembrance

We cannot begin to imagine the disgrace that childless Hannah must have felt. Year after year, she accompanied her husband Elkanah, his other wife Peninnah, and their children to worship at the tabernacle in Shiloh. Peninnah tormented Hannah with ridicule. The Bible tells us "her rival also provoked her severely, to make her miserable, because the Lord had closed her womb" (1 Samuel 1:6). Because this taunting went on year after year, Hannah's heart was so grieved that she couldn't eat. Elkanah's reassurance of his love and devotion was not enough. Hannah felt disgraced.

In desperation and despair, she prayed to God in tears at the tabernacle, making a vow that if God would only "look on the affliction of Your maidservant and remember me, and not forget Your maidservant" (1 Samuel 1:11), she would give that child to His service at the tabernacle. God looked at Hannah and remembered (1 Samuel 1:19). In due process of time, she became the mother of Samuel.

Nabal didn't think he needed any help from anyone; he felt no obligation to David.

Hannah remembered too. When her precious child was weaned, she took him to the tabernacle with an offering. How difficult it must have been to part with Samuel, but she had made a vow. She remembered that vow and gave her child to the Lord for a life of service.

Abigail Asked to Be Remembered

For ten years David and his band of followers darted from place to place in the wilderness as King Saul pursued them. But David and his men caused Nabal's workers no harm and even protected them as they cared for the sheep (1 Samuel 25:15–16). In return, David asked for supplies.

This wealthy man is described as being churlish and evil in his doings (1 Samuel 25:3 KJV). He didn't think he needed any help from anyone and felt no obligation to David. Not only did he refuse David's request, he also wrapped his reply in the greatest of insults:

> Who is David, and who is the son of Jesse? There are many servants nowadays who break away each one from his master. Shall I then take my bread and my water and my meat that I have killed for my shearers, and give it to men when I do not know where they are from? (1 Samuel 25:10–11).

David was furious and prepared to fight Nabal. His wife, Abigail, "a woman of good understanding and beautiful appearance" (1 Samuel 25:3), listened to the words of one of her husband's young men when he told her about the proposed attack.

Abigail was wise, realizing that actions usually speak louder than words. Sending servants ahead with abundant supplies, she slipped away from her husband on a donkey. When David first encountered Abigail, he was very angry. Falling down before him, she apologized for the behavior of her husband and asked for forgiveness. She then praised him and asked him to remember her when he became ruler over Israel (1 Samuel 25:31).

David did not wait to remember Abigail. He blessed her at that moment. When Nabal died shortly after this incident, David not only remembered Abigail—he married her!

Perhaps David's mercy at this time, as well as other incidents, prompted Solomon's petition many years later at the dedication of the temple: "O Lord God, do not turn away the face of Your Anointed; remember the mercies of Your servant David" (2 Chronicles 6:42).

Wise Words of Solomon

In the first chapter of Ecclesiastes, Solomon wrote about the vanity of earthly things. "There is no remembrance of former things, nor will there be any remembrance of things that are to come by those who will come after" (Ecclesiastes 1:11). He continued in the next chapter with some words about the folly of wisdom: "For there is no more remembrance of the wise than of the fool forever, since all that now is will be forgotten in the days to come. And how does a wise man die? As the fool!" (Ecclesiastes 2:16).

After many words concerning the vanities of life, David's wise son ended his writing with some advice to young people about what really mattered: "Remember now your Creator in the days of your youth, before the difficult days come, and the years draw near when you say, 'I have no pleasure in them'" (Ecclesiastes 12:1).

Nothing in this life is as important as remembering our Creator and making Him Lord of our lives. Solomon's concluding words were, "Let us hear the conclusion of the whole matter: fear God and keep His commandments, for this is man's all" (Ecclesiastes 12:13).

New Testament Examples

Mary's Memories

In the New Testament one of the first instances of saving special memories can be found in the second chapter of Luke. When Jesus was born in Bethlehem, an angel of the Lord appeared to some shepherds as they watched their flocks on the gently rolling hills surrounding the little town.

On that night the shepherds found the new-born baby, wrapped in swaddling clothes and lying in a manger, just as the heavenly messenger had said. Soon these common men spread the news of the announcement made to them concerning Jesus' birth. Their message reached far and wide.

Imagine seeing the world that night through Mary's eyes. She was a young teenage girl, married to Joseph, a common carpenter of Nazareth. From the beginning of her pregnancy, she had known that this was to be no ordinary child and neither was He conceived according to the natural laws of nature. At that time she was engaged to Joseph, but they had had no sexual union. Imagine the gossip of the town when it was learned that Mary was pregnant. In haste she fled to Elizabeth, an older relative who lived in Judea. That was a long journey for such a young girl! After staying with Elizabeth for a while, Mary returned to home to await the birth of her baby. Any sense of security must have been shattered when Caesar's decree concerning taxation was issued, mandating a journey to Bethlehem. It was almost time for her delivery!

So much happened to this very young girl in such a short time. The trip to Bethlehem had been a long and arduous one. Mary must have been anxious when they were turned away from the inn that night with only the offer of a stable to be shared with animals. Here, on a bed of straw with only Joseph to assist, the Son of God was born to a teenage girl. We can only wonder what her thoughts were at that moment—no grandparents to hold the new baby, no brothers, sisters, aunts, uncles, or other relatives. All alone Mary and Joseph rejoiced over the birth of their firstborn. We can only imagine their wonder when they heard some approaching footsteps in the night.

Imagine the gossip of the town when it was learned that Mary was pregnant.

As the shepherds one by one looked at the tiny baby, could Mary truly have comprehended the significance of their visit? Had the walls of the stable shielded the eyes of the new parents from the glory of the Lord that had shone around the shepherds when the angel made his appearance to them, or were they aware of something strange that happened on the Judean hillside? In the stillness of the night had they heard the voices of the multitude of the heavenly host praising God? Had they heard a commotion when the shepherds made their way into Bethlehem at that time of the night? What did Mary and Joseph think when a group of rugged men suddenly appeared at the entrance of the humble stable?

We tend to overlook the wrongs we have done to others, as if ignoring them will make them go away.

"But Mary kept all these things and pondered them in her heart" (Luke 2:19). In the years to come, the young mother had no photographs, no scrapbooks, no home movies, no videos, no DVDs but, oh, what memories were etched in her heart! She would never forget that night.

Remembering at the Altar

In Matthew 5:21–26 Jesus taught His followers a lesson concerning anger. Whereas the old law condemned killing, His new teaching made anger—the cause of so many murders—just as sinful as actually taking someone's life.

Jesus drove the point home by making an application to everyday life. If anyone brought a gift to the altar—a common occurrence—and remembered that a brother had something against him—he himself had sinned against that brother—he should go to that person and ask for forgiveness before finishing his worship.

All too often we tend to overlook, or even forget, the wrongs we have done to others, as if ignoring the hurts will make them go away. Christ said that we are to remember our wrongs and do something to make them right.

Titus Remembered the Obedience of the Corinthians

Paul discussed his joy over the repentance of the sinful members of the church at Corinth (2 Corinthians 7:13–16). Titus shared this same joy "because his spirit has been refreshed by you all" (v. 13). In verse 15 Paul further emphasized the depth of Titus' feelings by stating, "And his affections are greater for you as he remembers the obedience of you all, how with fear and trembling you received him." Nothing brings more joy to a gospel preacher than the memory of the obedience of people to the teachings of Christ.

Remembering the Thessalonians

In Paul's introductory remarks to the Thessalonian Christians, he stated that he, Silvanus, and Timothy were thankful for them, making mention of them in their prayers and "remembering without ceasing your work of faith, labor of love, and patience of hope in our Lord Jesus Christ in the sight of our God and Father, knowing, beloved brethren, your election by God" (1 Thessalonians 1:3–4).

Wouldn't it be rewarding if gospel preachers could remember the works of faith, the labors of love, and the patience of hope in the lives of all whom they had taught?

Conclusion

In this beginning chapter we have considered the importance of memory throughout the Bible. Students of His Word should stand in awe of the importance of the golden threads of memory and ponder their lessons just as Mary did on that night so long ago.

Questions for Thought

1. What was God's covenant with Noah and his sons? (Genesis 9:11). What was to be the visual reminder of this covenant between Jehovah and mankind? (Genesis 9:16).

2. How could the butler have forgotten his promise to Joseph? (Genesis 40:23). If you had been Joseph, how would you have felt?

3. For what two reasons were the Jews told to remember the Sabbath day and keep it holy? (Exodus 20:11; Deuteronomy 5:15).

4. In Deuteronomy 9:6–29, the Israelites were told to remember their rebellion against God. In what ways had they rebelled? In this context, what had Moses asked Jehovah to remember?

5. What did the Feast of Weeks help the Jews to remember? (Deuteronomy 16:12).

6. The remembrance of the Israelites' slavery in Egypt was to prompt their merciful treatment of what groups of people? (Deuteronomy 24:17–18, 22).

7. What was the purpose of the fringes on the garments of the Jews? (Numbers 15:38–40).

8. In the Deuteronomy 6, how were parents to help their children remember the word of God? What were they first to do before they attempted to teach their children?

9. Why were the Jews to remember what God did to Miriam? (Deuteronomy 24:9).

10. As Moses stood on Mount Nebo to view the promised land, what thoughts must have run through his mind? (Deuteronomy 34:1–8).

11. The stones at Gilgal were to remind the people of what two events? (Joshua 4:1–24). What is the value of memorials or other visual reminders?

12. Describe the circumstances under which Samson asked God to remember him (Judges 16:28).

13. Why did God remember Hannah? (1 Samuel 1:1–28). How did Hannah remember her promise to God?

14. What prompted Abigail's request that David would remember her when he became king? (1 Samuel 25:1–42).

15. What is the reasoning behind the admonition to remember the Creator in the days of youth? (Ecclesiastes 12:1).

16. Try putting yourself in Mary's place and then describe the events that she undoubtedly pondered in her heart on the night Jesus was born (Luke 2:19).

17. If a person goes to worship and remembers that someone else has something against him, what is he first to do? (Matthew 5:21–26).

18. What remembrance brought joy to Titus? (2 Corinthians 7:15).

19. What good things did Paul, Silvanus, and Timothy remember about the Thessalonians? (1 Thessalonians 1:3–4).

Jane, age 6, with mom
Elma Delk Shannon

Jane, 9 months

Jane, age 3

Old letter and postcard from
memorabila

Remembering: The Passover

One night in Jewish history was so special that God commanded it to become a yearly remembrance. The Passover had its origin in Egypt over four hundred years after Jacob and his offspring made their way into a strange place when famine had devastated their own land.

In our Bible classes sometimes we discuss the facts but fail to even begin to fathom the emotions of that night of deliverance. As a young girl I was blessed with a teacher who had the ability to make each of the characters step out of the written pages and seem so real that I could almost feel the sand in my own shoes as we traced the footsteps of God's people in Egypt and the wilderness.

In this chapter we will gain not only a mastery of the facts surrounding this momentous occasion but we will also experience the emotions that must have accompanied the events of that night thousands of years ago.

A Privileged Race

Approximately 430 years prior to the Passover, both the forgiveness of Joseph and his unfailing love for his family had saved them from starvation and provided them with a choice piece of land in Egypt: "You meant evil against me; but God meant it for good, in order to bring it about as it is this day, to save many people alive" (Genesis 50:20).

Because Joseph held an office equivalent to a Prime Minister (second only to the Pharaoh), Jacob, his sons, and their families were treated well in Egypt. For a time, they lived as a privileged race with their own tribal leaders, customs, and religion.

Reduced to Slavery

A few generations later, however, the Israelites found that they were no longer welcome in their adopted land. At the time of their departure, their number had grown from seventy souls (Exodus 1:5) to more than a million—600 thousand men on foot in addition to their wives, children, and the older people who could not walk (Exodus 12:37).

A new king "who did not know Joseph" had come into power (Exodus 1:8). Fearing because the Israelites were more and mightier than they were and could easily join forces with an enemy to defeat Egypt (Exodus 1:9–10), the rulers decided upon a course of action that would weaken the Israelites and keep the growth of these foreigners in check. The special rights and privileges of the Israelites no longer existed, as they were reduced to the status of slaves, who provided the labor to build treasure cities for the Egyptians. The land of Goshen, the Egyptian home to the descendents of Jacob, began just a few miles south of the new capital and stretched as far as Pithom. How convenient it was to drag the Israelites away from their flocks and force them into servitude.

Often we read the words about slavery in the first chapter of Exodus but fail to reflect upon the wretchedness of the lives of the Israelites. Twenty-four hours a day, a slave's life belonged to his master. From the time he awakened in the morning until he fell asleep exhausted at night in his humble dwelling, he did whatever his taskmaster demanded. The Egyptians would "afflict them with their burdens" (Exodus 1:11).

Affliction meant beatings with cruel whips if slaves failed to complete their back-breaking assignments. They moved gargantuan boulders in the blazing sun day in and day out. Scriptures depict their wretched condition with phrases such as:

> The more they afflicted them, the more they multiplied and grew . . . they were in dread of the children of Israel . . . the Egyptians made the children of Israel serve with rigor . . . they made their lives bitter with hard bondage—in mortar, in brick, and in all manner of service in the field. All their service in which they made them serve was with rigor (Exodus 1:12–14).

First, the Israelites had to dig the clay and then they had to form it into bricks that were dried in the hot Egyptian sun. Then they had to carry these materials to the places where buildings were being constructed. But the more God's people were oppressed, the more they multiplied (Exodus 1:12). Pharaoh needed a new strategy.

Kill the Baby Boys!

Not only were the Egyptians cruel in their physical treatment of the Jewish slaves, but they also began to tug at the heartstrings of these people in bondage. In an effort to reduce the Israelites in number, the king ordered the midwives to kill all the Jewish males at birth. Refusing to carry out the king's commands, the midwives excused their actions by asserting that the strong Hebrew women delivered easily before help could arrive. When the Pharaoh could not diminish the Israelite population through the midwives, he proclaimed a royal decree. Every Israelite male child was to be thrown into the Nile!

We often tell the story of Moses in the basket without stopping to reflect upon the utter panic an Israelite mother must have felt at the moment she gave birth. These horrible events took place long before the revelations of ultrasound. When a woman's labor pains began, she had no way of knowing whether her baby would be male or female. Bonding takes place the moment a mother sees and holds her newborn baby and hears those first cries. If her baby happened to be a girl, she could breathe a sigh of relief. If it were a boy, however, she must have had mixed feelings: joy over having given birth to her baby, mingled with the dread of having him killed. How could any parents tolerate the emotional pain of having their baby snatched from their arms? How did they feel when they heard his cries silenced by the waters of the Nile? Day in and day out this bone-chilling slaughter continued.

Every Israelite male child was to be thrown into the Nile! How could parents tolerate their baby being snatched from their arms?

Save My Baby!

In desperation Jochebed, the wife of Amram of the tribe of Levi, defied the Egyptian royal decree by hiding her newborn son for three months. Try to imagine her terror as, day in and day out, she heard the footsteps of the Egyptian soldiers when they entered her neighbors' houses and then the cries of the babies around her as they were taken by force and thrown into the Nile. Babies cannot be kept from crying. What fear must have come over Jochebed each time her baby uttered a sound.

By the time Moses was three months old, he could no longer be hidden. Devising a scheme to save his life, Jochebed placed her baby in an ark made of bulrushes and daubed it with slime and pitch. Try to imagine her feelings on the day she put Moses in that little boat and set him loose on the Nile River, protected only by the watchful eye of his sister, Miriam. Every Bible student knows that Pharaoh's daughter discovered the ark and had compassion on the baby. Because of Miriam's intercession, young Moses was allowed to remain with his own mother for quite some time. Eventually, he was adopted into the royal family.

Affliction with the People of God

God was aware of the oppression of the Israelite slaves. They needed someone to intercede for them. That leader had been born, but he was not yet ready for such a task. More than thirty years in Pharaoh's palace educated Moses in secular learning and offered many advantages, but he must have grown resentful of the Egyptians' treatment of his own people. Daily he heard the sound of a taskmaster's whip and the cries of his kinsmen. The writer of Hebrews tells us: "By faith Moses, when he became of age, refused to be called the son of Pharaoh's daughter, choosing rather to suffer affliction with the people of God than to enjoy the passing pleasures of sin" (Hebrews 11:24–25).

Moses resorted to violence by killing an Egyptian taskmaster who was mistreating a Hebrew slave. Possibly the incident would have gone unnoticed had Moses not tried to settle a dispute the next day between two Israelites. When an angry Israelite challenged the right of Pharaoh's adopted grandson to intervene and mentioned the slain Egyptian, Moses knew he had to flee from Egypt. From that moment his life was changed. Because Canaan was occupied by Egypt, Moses escaped to the mountains of Midian, east of the Gulf of Aqubah, where he spent the next forty years as a shepherd.

God had a plan. A leader was being hewn out of the rugged land of Midian and shaped for the tremendous task of leading a nation of people out of bondage.

The Scriptures give no indication that the Egyptians were treating their slaves any better forty years later than when Moses witnessed the mistreatment of his people

With the death of the Pharaoh, who was the ruler over Egypt at the time Moses killed the Egyptian (Exodus 2:23), Israel must have hoped for deliverance from the oppression. Jehovah heard their cries and groaning and remembered His covenant with Abraham, Isaac, and Jacob (Exodus 2:23–25).

It was against this background that God appeared to Moses in a burning bush to persuade the reluctant shepherd to return to Egypt and lead his people out of slavery and back to their homeland.

Let My People Go!

One can only imagine the thoughts that must have run through the mind of Moses as he and his brother Aaron entered the majestic palace where Moses had spent most of his youth. When the adopted grandson of the former Pharaoh demanded, "Let my people go" to observe a feast in the wilderness, the Egyptian ruler scoffed at the request of a slave and an insignificant shepherd from Midian: "Who *is* the Lord, that I should obey His voice to let Israel go? I do not know the Lord, nor will I let Israel go" (Exodus 5:2). No ruler would want to give up a cheap supply of forced foreign labor.

Not only did Pharaoh refuse to let the Israelites leave the country to observe a feast, he also made their tasks even more difficult! Previously the workers had been given straw to be used as a binding material in the making of bricks. Now they were ordered to find their own stubble while being expected to produce the same amount of bricks.

Dejected, Moses questioned God about sending him to be a deliverer. Jehovah assured him that deliverance was at hand. The two brothers once again appeared before the Egyptian ruler. When Aaron cast down the rod that had been given him as a symbol of God's authority and power, the rod became a serpent. The court magicians performed a similar feat in an attempt to discredit the two Israelites. Jehovah, however, demonstrated His power over the Egyptians when Aaron's serpent swallowed their serpents (Exodus 7:12).

The Hand of God

- When Pharaoh refused to acknowledge the claims of Jehovah, the entire land suffered a series of ten plagues. First, Moses stretched his rod over the Nile, causing the waters to turn to blood, thus causing the fish to die and stink (Exodus 7:14–25). This first plague lasted for seven days, but Pharaoh remained unmoved.

- The next time it was Aaron who stretched his rod over the waters, and an army of frogs invaded the land (Exodus 8:1–15). They were everywhere: in their beds, in their ovens, and even in their kneading troughs! Pharaoh's magicians also produced frogs, covering the land. When Moses cried unto the Lord, the frogs died, causing a terrible stench. Pharaoh still refused.

- When Moses smote the ground with his rod, lice appeared on both the people and the animals (Exodus 8:16–19). The court magicians had been successful in imitating the first two plagues but this time they failed, reporting to Pharaoh: "This is the finger of God" (Exodus 8:19). He still refused to let God's people go.

- During the fourth plague (Exodus 8:20–32), for the first time the Israelites were spared. Pesky flies covered the rest of the land but not in Goshen, where God's people lived (Exodus 8:22–23). Pharaoh begged to have the flies taken away, promising the Israelites permission to travel into the wilderness to sacrifice. When the plague was lifted, however, the ruler once again refused to let the slaves leave.

- The fifth plague (Exodus 9:1–7) affected Egypt's religion as well as her economic life. For centuries the Apis Bull had been an object of veneration to these pagans. All the cattle of the Egyptians died, but God's people did not lose a single one. Still Pharaoh refused.

- The sixth plague (Exodus 9:8–12) afflicted both animals and humans with painful boils. Again the plague was restricted to the Egyptians. Pharaoh refused once more.

- God used a disastrous hailstorm as the seventh plague (Exodus 9:18–35), killing both man and beast in the field, as well as vegetation. "Only in the land of Goshen, where the children of Israel were, was there no hail" (Exodus 9:26). It was during this plague that Pharaoh acknowledged his sinfulness in failing to let Israel go and asked Moses to entreat the Lord to stop the storms. When the thunder and hail ceased, however, Pharaoh said no.

- Once again Aaron and Moses stood before Pharaoh with the pronouncement of an eighth plague (Exodus 10:1–20). Locusts would invade the land, destroying whatever vegetation had been left after the previous plagues, if Pharaoh refused to let the Israelites leave. Growing weary—"How long shall this man be a snare to us?"—the Egyptian ruler told them to go serve their God but asked them who planned to make this journey to worship. When Moses told him that all the people, along with their flocks and herds, were going to travel, Pharaoh balked. He wanted to release only the men because he knew they would return to their families instead of escaping from Egypt. The ruler's proposal was totally unacceptable, and again the rod of Moses brought a plague. This time locusts covered the face of the earth, eating every green plant. Pharaoh repented until the plague had been lifted. Then he refused one more time.

In the ninth plague a thick darkness covered the land for three days (Exodus 10:21–29). The blackness was so dense that the Egyptians could not leave their houses, but the Israelites had light in their dwellings. This time Pharaoh gave permission for all the people to journey into the wilderness to serve their god, but the animals would have to stay behind. Moses refused, explaining that the beasts would be needed for sacrifices. Previous to this occasion, the Egyptian ruler had left the door open for negotiations. However, this time he closed any avenue for future communication, threatening Moses with death if he ever again attempted to come into his presence.

Pharaoh would soon feel the hand of God as he had never felt it before.

Moses' parting words were portentous: "You have spoken well. I will never see your face again" (Exodus 10:29). But Pharaoh would soon feel the hand of God as he had never felt it before. One more plague was forthcoming. It is hereafter remembered in the observance of the Passover.

The Tenth Plague Foretold

There Shall Be a Great Cry in Egypt

Although the Hebrews had escaped the ravages of most of the plagues, they were well aware of what had been happening in the land of Egypt. The Scriptures say nothing about God's people being spared from the consequences of the bloody waters of the Nile. We assume they also had frogs in their beds and ovens. Neither are we told that they had no lice. Beginning with the plague of flies, however, God's people were spared, but they undoubtedly were aware of the events taking place in the rest of Egypt: the swarms of flies, the death of the cattle, the boils, the devastating hail, and the overpowering darkness. Nothing had moved Pharaoh. The Israelites must have wondered if they would ever leave Egypt!

Through Moses the Lord announced that He would go out into the midst of Egypt and the firstborn in every family would die, from the oldest child of Pharaoh himself to the lowest maid-servant, and even to the firstborn of beasts. "Then there shall be a great cry throughout all the land of Egypt, such as was not like it before, nor shall be like it again" (Exodus 11:6). The first-born in *every* family in Egypt would die, as well as the firstborn of the animals.

The bloody Nile, the nuisance of frogs being in every place, the itching of lice, flies swarming and crawling all over the people day and night, the economic devastation from losing cattle, the pain of boils covering their bodies, the destruction of hail-storms and locusts, and the pitch black of darkness that covered the land for three days—all had been horrible. But nothing could compare to the prospect of the loss of one's own flesh and blood. "Then there shall be a great cry throughout all the land of Egypt, such as was not like it before, nor shall be like it again" (Exodus 11:6).

God's Orders

Even the prospect of this final plague could not persuade Pharaoh to let the Israelites leave. He had made his decision and the course of events began taking shape for that final destruction.

Exodus 12:1–14 records God's commands:

1. The month of deliverance would henceforth be regarded as the first month of the Jewish year.

2. The lamb to be used on this occasion would be taken from the flock on the tenth day of that month.

3. The blemish-free lamb had to be separated from the flock and kept up until the fourteenth day of that month. Every household in Israel would kill its lamb in the evening of that day.

4. If a household proved to be too small to consume an entire lamb, two small families could combine for the feast.

5. Every household would sprinkle the blood of that lamb on the two side posts of the house as well as on the upper door post.

6. That same night the lamb would be roasted whole with fire and all of it eaten, along with unleavened bread and bitter herbs. Any uneaten part would be burned with fire.

7. Instead of relaxing, the people were to eat with their belts on their waists, ready for travel. (When people journeyed in Bible times, they usually tucked the front part of their long, loose garments under the girdle, or belt, that they wore around their waists.)

8. They were to eat with their staffs in their hands, ready to depart.

9. Instead of removing their shoes for the meal as they customarily did, the Israelites were told to leave them on and be ready to travel at any minute.

10. They were to eat in haste because the Lord was at hand.

After pronouncing the name of this new observance as the *Passover*, God told His people He would pass through Egypt that night and kill the firstborn of every family and also of the beasts. The blood that was sprinkled on the doorposts of the Jewish homes would mark their dwellings and God would pass over those houses.

A Memorial before the Memory

Even before the lambs were killed, Jehovah proclaimed that *that* particular night—when God would pass over their homes—would remain as a memorial throughout their generations (Exodus 12:14). It was so important that it was designated as a memorial even before there was a memory to keep.

Immediately following God's instructions for observing the Passover, He told them how to observe another ordinance: the Feast of Unleavened Bread, which was to begin on the day following the Passover and was to last seven days for the purpose of sanctifying every firstborn (Exodus 12:15–20). During that time, no leaven was allowed in the homes of God's people. If anyone did not take God's command seriously, that person was to be cast out from the congregation of Israel. (Because the Passover and the Feast of Unleavened Bread were observed back to back, they became one eight-day religious festival.)

If anyone did not take God's command seriously, they were cast out from the congregation.

Before the Passover was even prepared, Moses informed the people that this special day of deliverance was to be observed throughout their history. He even told them what to tell their children in the years to come when they asked about the meaning of the Passover:

> That you shall say, "It is the Passover sacrifice of the Lord, who passed over the houses of the children of Israel in Egypt when He struck the Egyptians and delivered our households" (Exodus 12:27).

Exodus 12:28 summarized what happened by stating: "Then the children of Israel went away and did so; just as the Lord had commanded Moses and Aaron, so they did."

The Deliverance

A Great Cry—None Like It

The darkness of evening found the people in every Jewish home wearing their traveling clothes and hastily eating their final meal—roasted lamb, unleavened bread, and bitter herbs. Probably they ate while standing and with little conversation. We can only wonder what their feelings were, when at midnight they heard the distant wails of the first family that had lost its oldest child. Cries went up from every Egyptian house and soon the entire land was in deep sorrow. "Then there shall be a great cry throughout all the land of Egypt, such as was not like it before, nor shall be like it again" (Exodus 11:6).

Even the royal palace was not spared. In the darkness of night, when Pharaoh discovered that his own son was dead—just as Moses had predicted—the mighty ruler called for the two leaders of his slaves and commanded them to lead *all* the Israelites from the country with *all* their flocks and cattle. He wanted nothing else to do with these foreigners who had brought so much torment to him and his empire. The Egyptians, deep in sorrow over the loss of their children, joined with their ruler in urging the Israelites to leave with haste.

Flee with Your Dough Board

It is difficult to imagine the sight of that many people and animals leaving Egypt so hurriedly. More than a million Israelites were fleeing with all their flocks and herds, carrying the jewels of silver and gold, in addition the clothes they had borrowed from the Egyptians. They also carried something rather strange. Each household had a kneading trough—dough board—for mixing and kneading bread. The people were commanded to place that dough board, along with a lump of unleavened bread, on their shoulders and tucked in the folds of their clothing. Imagine fleeing in haste with a dough board on your shoulder!

The next day when this strange looking group finally reached safety, they stopped and baked their lumps of unleavened bread, which was to become a symbol of purged sin throughout future generations.

Conclusion

"A Memorial between Thine Eyes"

As a young child, under the direction of one Bible teacher, I memorized the ten plagues. I suppose being able to recite them has merit. As I mentioned earlier, however, I was blessed with another teacher who helped me learn to step into the shoes of the Bible characters in our studies. I will forever be grateful to her.

We have no way of knowing what went through the minds of God's people on that first day of freedom as they ate the only bread they had: the lumps of unleavened bread they had snatched before they left. (This was the beginning day of what would henceforth be known as the Feast of Unleavened Bread, which would last for seven days following the observance of the Passover.)

If I had been among those people, I believe I would have thought about the recent sounds of Egyptian whips on the backs of my loved ones, the earlier drowning of male babies, our poverty, and wondering if we would ever be free again. I would probably have reflected upon the undrinkable water from the Nile, the frogs that had been in my house (and the stench when they died), and the torment of the itching lice. I would have remembered the reports about what had happened to the Egyptians: the tormenting flies, their cattle dying, their painful boils, the unrelenting storms and hail, the locusts, and the overwhelming darkness.

Most of all, I would probably have reflected upon my family's last meal in Egypt on the previous night as we had eaten the roasted lamb, the unleavened bread, and the bitter herbs.

Although I had dressed for flight that evening and had eaten my meal in haste, no doubt at that time I would have wondered if this last plague would really change Pharaoh's mind. When I had heard the screams of the Egyptians as they found their firstborn children dead, I could have questioned whether or not the blood sprinkled on our house would really spare my own firstborn. I would never forget hurrying my family out of our house and rounding up our animals to join the thousands of people and livestock making their way out of Egypt.

God wanted His people to always keep the memories of that night and the following events fresh in their minds, even long after those who had participated in the flight from their captivity had passed away. No doubt they remembered the earlier words of Moses.

And thou shalt show thy son in that day, saying,

"This is done because of what the Lord did for me when I came up from Egypt." It shall be as a sign to you on your hand and as a memorial between your eyes, that the Lord's law may be in your mouth; for with a strong hand the Lord has brought you out of Egypt. You shall therefore keep this ordinance in its season from year to year (Exodus 13:8–10).

God's Mercy or Egypt's Food?—Choose Your Memories

Although the details of the keeping of the Passover and the Feast of Unleavened Bread changed throughout the years, God wanted His people always to remember.

As horrible as the captivity had been and as wonderful as their freedom must have seemed at that moment, it was not too long before they forgot God's mercy in His deliverance. In the first month of the second year after they had come out of the land of Egypt, Moses again reminded the people of the observance of the Passover and the Feast of Unleavened Bread (Numbers 9:1–14). Shortly after this instruction, the Israelites failed to remember their miraculous deliverance from slavery. Instead, they wept as they cried for the fish, the cucumbers, the melons, the leeks, the onions, and the garlic of Egypt (Numbers 11:4–6). We must choose our memories wisely.

Questions for Thought

1. According to Genesis 50:20, what good resulted from the betrayal of Joseph by his brothers?

2. Why did the Egyptian rulers make the Israelites their slaves? (Exodus 1:9). Describe the conditions of slavery (Exodus 1:11–14: Exodus 2:23–24).

3. Why wasn't the first plan to reduce the number of the Israelites through the agents of the midwives successful? (Exodus 1:15–21). To what drastic means did Pharaoh then resort? (Exodus 1:22).

4. Relate the events of the first 40 years of the life of Moses (Exodus 2:1–15).

5. Do you think Moses was ready to lead his people at age 40? Why was he selected at age 80? What had happened in the intervening years?

6. What five excuses did Moses make in an effort to avoid asking for the deliverance of the Israelites? (Exodus 3:11–4:17).

7. How do you think Moses must have felt when he first entered the palace where he had spent his younger years?

8. Briefly describe each of the first nine plagues (Exodus 7:14–10:29).

9. How did the magicians of Egypt also have the power to turn the river into blood (Exodus 7:22) and cause frogs to appear? (Exodus 8:7). Earlier, how could they have made their rods turn into serpents? (Exodus 7:8–12).

10. Why was the heart of Pharaoh repeatedly hardened?

11. List the instructions that God gave through Moses for the observance of the Passover (Exodus 12:1–14, 43–49).

12. Distinguish between the Passover and the Feast of Unleavened Bread (Exodus 12:15–20).

13. Not only did Jehovah proclaim that the Passover would be kept as a memory (Exodus 12:14), but He also gave instructions for generations yet to come. What were the children who were yet unborn to be told? (Exodus 12:26–27; Exodus 13:8–10).

14. Try to step into the shoes of a typical Israelite on the night of the tenth plague. Describe what he probably saw and what he must have felt.

15. Why were the Israelites commanded to carry their kneading troughs and their lumps of unleavened bread with them as they fled? (Exodus 12:34).

16. According to Exodus 13:19, what else did the Israelites take with them?

17. On that first day of deliverance, as the Israelites pulled out their dough boards and baked their unleavened bread for their first meal of freedom, what thoughts must have gone through their minds?

18. Shortly after the observance of the Passover in the first month of the second year out of captivity (Numbers 9:1–14), the Israelites apparently had forgotten the wretchedness of their slavery. What did they ask for in Numbers 11:4–6?

19. Do you think you would have been any different?

20. Do some research on the changes in the observance of the Passover throughout the years.

Don preaching on the radio, 1967

Jane, 1968

Jane (2nd from left) Class Treasurer, Lipscomb

Old postcard from memorabilia

Remembering: The Lord's Supper

For more than fifteen hundred years, the Israelites had been pausing once each year to remember their deliverance from Egyptian bondage by observing the Passover. On this occasion of remembering, with the family gathered around the roasted lamb, the unleavened bread, and the bitter herbs, the head of each household carefully explained the significance of the feast to the younger generation to keep the memory of that night in Egypt forever etched in their hearts.

The Jews needed to remember God's deliverance, but the Passover had another purpose. It was a foreshadow of a new feast that would be observed until the end of time. "Therefore the law was our tutor to bring us to Christ, that we might be justified by faith" (Galatians 3:24). For over fifteen hundred years, God had been teaching His chosen people that remembering was important. Now the fullness of time had come, the time for Him to offer spiritual deliverance to the entire world, Jews and Gentiles alike. Paul expressed the beauty of God's deliverance in the following words:

> For you are all sons of God through faith in Christ Jesus. For as many of you as were baptized into Christ have put on Christ.

There is neither Jew nor Greek, there is neither slave nor free, there is neither male nor female; for you are all one in Christ Jesus (Galatians 3:26–28).

Events Leading to the Lord's Supper

A Busy Week

The days immediately preceding the establishment of the Lord's supper had been filled with activity. Leaving Jericho, Jesus and His apostles made their way toward Jerusalem and the last week before His crucifixion.

The multitudes were supportive. When the Lord made His triumphant entry into His beloved Jerusalem on the back of a common beast of burden, the people thronged His path, spreading their clothes and branches before Him.

The people thronged His path, spreading their clothes and branches before Him.

Going into the temple, Jesus displayed His authority by overthrowing the tables of the money-changers, as well as the seats of those who sold doves. He also verbally rebuked their misuse of God's house.

That evening Christ left Jerusalem, resorting to the neighboring village of Bethany, where His dear friends Mary, Martha, and Lazarus lived. During the last week before His death, it seems that Jesus and His followers spent their nights in Bethany but the activities of many of their daytime hours, however, revolved around the metropolis of Jerusalem.

During this time, the Master cursed the barren fig tree, answered questions about His authority, told a number of parables, and taught lessons about the importance of paying taxes to Caesar, as well as the nature of the resurrection. He reprimanded the hypocrisy of the scribes and Pharisees and then wept over Jerusalem because of her failure to listen to Him.

In connection with His deep sorrow over His beloved city, the Lord prophesied her destruction. During all of Jesus' activities, the chief priests, the scribes, and the elders had been plotting against this man who challenged their authority. During the evening of one of these final days, Christ was anointed in Bethany at the house of Simon the leper. Then Judas left Christ and the apostles so he could meet with the chief priests. What a busy week it had been!

The Master's Orders

On Thursday of that eventful week, Jesus' disciples asked Him where they should make preparations for the observance of the Passover. Obeying the Master's instructions, Peter and John followed a man bearing a pitcher of water—a rather unusual sight in those days when women normally carried the water (Luke 22:8). After requesting permission from the master of the house to use his guest chamber, they were shown to a large upper room. Here they began making preparations for the observance of that feast dedicated to the remembrance of their ancestors' deliverance from Egypt. Jesus and His apostles did not allow their busy schedule to hinder their observance of this important feast.

The Supper

Lay Aside the Shadow

A room had been secured. The lamb had been roasted and all the other food for the Passover had been prepared when Jesus and the remainder of His apostles made their way through the crowded streets of Jerusalem near sunset to their designated meeting place. As they assembled at the table, Jesus told them He desired to eat the Passover with them before He suffered. Then He remarked, "I will no longer eat of it until it is fulfilled in the kingdom of God" (Luke 22:16). The Passover was fulfilled when Christ was sacrificed for us (1 Corinthians 5:7). The shadow of the Passover would be laid aside in the kingdom because the substance, the real sacrifice of the Lamb of God, would take the place of all those bloody lambs.

The Greatest in the Kingdom

Even after three years of association with the Master, the apostles were slow to comprehend the nature of the spiritual kingdom yet to come. At this solemn occasion, a contention arose among the twelve about which of them would be the greatest.

Jesus knew His followers needed an object lesson on humility. Quietly arising from His reclining position during supper, the Lord removed His outer clothing and wrapped a towel around His waist. After pouring water into a basin, the Master proceeded to wash His disciples' feet and dry them with the towel. At first, impulsive Peter protested, but then he relented saying, "Lord, not my feet only, but also my hands and my head!" (John 13:9).

My Body, My Blood

In that upper room a new memorial feast was about to be instituted. Taking the unleavened bread that had been on the table for the Passover, Jesus blessed it, broke it, and then gave it to the disciples, saying, "Take, eat; this is My body" (Matthew 26:26). After giving thanks for the cup, He gave it to them saying, "Drink from it, all of you. For this is My blood of the new covenant, which is shed for many for the remission of sins" (Matthew 26:27–28).

The apostles still did not completely understand the spiritual nature of the kingdom Jesus was about to establish. They probably did not even have a clue about the significance of the unleavened bread and the cup when He told them to partake of it in remembrance of Him (Luke 22:19). After all, Christ was going to set up a kingdom. Some of them had been seeking places of honor in that kingdom. Unleavened bread representing their Master's body? The fruit of the vine representing His blood? He wasn't supposed to shed His blood and certainly not to lose His life. After all, He was to be a triumphant ruler; they were under the impression they would reign with Him.

Whether or not the apostles completely understood the significance of the last supper, that night Christ was replacing the Passover with a new spiritual feast. The unleavened bread, used in the Passover and signifying the absence of sin, was again selected. This time it would represent His sinless body. The fruit of the vine was to remind the followers of Christ of the blood He shed on the cross. Instead of the sacrifice of a lamb without blemish, there would now be a one-time supreme sacrifice of the perfect lamb, the Son of God. These two emblems would help Christians remember His supreme sacrifice. During the hundreds of years of the observance of the Passover, no sins were paid for; they were remembered each year. Now, because of Jesus' sacrifice, sins are removed forever.

His disciples had no idea what potential memories were waiting for them.

Memorial before Memories

Just as the Passover was instituted as a memorial before there were any memories of the event, so was the Lord's supper observed before there were any memories of the death of Christ.

When the group in that upper room had sung a hymn, they left with Jesus in the darkness of the night as He continued His final discourse on the way to a special place on the Mount of Olives. His disciples had no idea what potential memories were waiting for them. Because of God's inspired writers, however, we have a complete record of those happenings to help us remember. Just as the early Christians assembled on the first day of the week to break bread (Acts 20:7) and remember the sacrifice Christ had made for their sins, we also assemble upon the first day of the week and reflect upon the events of those days so long ago. At each observance we should step into the shoes of Christ and His followers as we vicariously retrace their steps, experiencing what they saw and feeling their emotions.

In the Garden

Jesus Sweats Blood

Because of the observance of the Passover and the Feast of Unleavened Bread, Jerusalem was teeming with Jews from other towns. Jesus and His little band of followers left the upper room, made their way through the crowded streets, and crossed the Kidron Valley to a familiar place on the Mount of Olives: the Garden of Gethsemane.

Jesus left eight of the apostles near the entrance with instructions to wait there. (From this vantage point, they could see a long distance and be aware of danger.) Christ went further into the garden with Peter, James, and John. After telling these three to stay at a certain place, Jesus walked into the blackness of the night by Himself before He poured out His heart to His Father as He begged, "Abba, Father, all things are possible for You. Take this cup away from Me; nevertheless, not what I will, but what You will" (Mark 14:36).

Sometimes we mistakenly picture the image of a serene, confident person in the garden, but Hebrews 5:7 states that Christ prayed "with vehement cries and tears to Him who was able to save Him from death." Luke 22:43–44 adds that, even though an angel from heaven strengthened Him, He was in anguish and prayed more earnestly, His sweat like drops of blood falling to the ground. Christ was not sweating because of the heat. The Passover is always in the early spring. Later that night it was cool enough for a fire in the courtyard of the high priest. Our Lord was living in a human body and was sweating because of tremendous stress.

Light is shed on the hours before and during the crucifixion of Jesus from a medical point of view on pages 1455–1463 of the March 21, 1986, issue of the *Journal of the American Medical Association*. Although the condition is rare, a bloody sweat can occur in highly emotional situations when blood seeps into the sweat glands with the skin becoming fragile and tender.

"Sleeping for Sorrow"

Returning to Peter, James, and John and finding them asleep, Jesus chided these three apostles for not being able to stay awake for one hour. However, Luke the physician had insight into the cause of their drowsiness: "He found them sleeping from sorrow" (Luke 22:45). How bewildered these three men must have been as they waited in that lonely garden, unable to comprehend what was happening. All who have experienced depression caused by sorrow can understand its debilitating effects.

> *In highly emotional situations, blood seeps into the sweat glands— the skin becomes fragile and tender.*

Two more times the Lord left Peter, James, and John while He implored the Father to spare Him from the upcoming ordeal. Two more times the silence of God whispered no through the trees in the garden.

Kiss of Betrayal

Judas had begun his treason earlier by plotting with the Jewish officials after Christ was anointed at the house of Simon the leper. After being offered thirty pieces of silver, he began looking for opportunities to betray the Master (Matthew 26:14–16). Earlier that evening in the upper room, after Jesus had handed Judas a piece of bread that He had dipped in the dish, the traitor slipped away from the other apostles to finalize his diabolical plot. At this moment he was making his way from

Jerusalem with a detachment of temple soldiers and Jewish religious leaders to a familiar place where Jesus and His apostles had often resorted.

The torches and lanterns pierced the night's darkness as Judas and his followers entered the grove, prompting Jesus to say to His apostles, "Rise, let us be going. See, My betrayer is at hand" (Mark 14:42). But Christ did not try to run away. Instead, He confronted this militant band of men face to face.

Try to imagine what a commotion Judas and the rest of the crowd must have made as they wound their way from Jerusalem, down the slope to the Kidron Valley, and up to the garden, or grove, on the Mount of Olives. Because of the terrain, their lights could be seen for quite a distance. Not only did they have torches and lanterns but they also had weapons, swords, and clubs to overpower an unarmed carpenter from Galilee, along with a small band composed primarily of fishermen. What a sight!

These spiritually immature apostles may have reasoned that He could never become king without someone to fight for Him.

Matthew, Mark, and Luke relate that after Judas identified Jesus by the prearranged signal of a kiss, one of His apostles cut off the right ear of a servant of the high priest. Try to imagine the electrically charged atmosphere at that moment when Jesus healed the man and rebuked His apostle for using a sword. After all, had not Christ only recently commanded the apostles to sell their garments and buy swords? And when they indicated they had two swords He said, "It is enough" (Luke 22:36–38). So these spiritually immature apostles may have reasoned that He could never become king without someone to fight for Him.

Bound and Charged

John's account omits the kiss of Judas but relates that Jesus took control of the situation by calmly asking, "Whom are you seeking?" (John 18:4). When He was told they were looking for Jesus of Nazareth, the Lord stated simply but powerfully, "I am He" (John 18:5). That moment was also charged with tension as the large company of soldiers and Jewish religious leaders suddenly fell to the ground. We often hurriedly read those words in the Scriptures without pausing to reflect upon the magnitude of the event: strong, armed men falling down for no apparent reason!

According to John, once more Jesus asked His accusers whom they were seeking, only to receive the same answer. And again He replied, "I have told you that I am He. Therefore, if you seek Me, let these go their way" (John 18:8). John placed the incident of the attack on the servant of the high priest as happening immediately after the men had fallen to the ground, identifying Peter as the one with the sword and Malchus as the servant of the high priest (John 18:10).

Mark tells us that a young man, wearing nothing but a linen garment, fled when they seized Jesus, leaving his garment behind (Mark 14:51–52). Some scholars think this was John Mark.

As if this carpenter from Galilee were a common criminal, the soldiers bound His hands and led Him through the stillness of the night to begin the legal process of taking His life. Although He could have called twelve legions of angels to deliver Him, He chose to submit (Matthew 26:53).

The Trials

Between the blackness of the early morning hours (approximately 12:30–1:00 A.M. until 9:00 A.M.), Jesus suffered the ordeal of a number of trials, as well as extreme physical pain.

The Jewish trial consisted of three stages. First, there was the informal examination by Annas, the ex-high priest and the father-in-law of Caiaphas, while the Sanhedrin—the Jewish governing body—was assembling. Next there was the hurried trial by the Sanhedrin while it was still night, and then the official legal condemnation by the Sanhedrin after dawn.

Before Annas

First Christ was taken to Annas for a Jewish inquisition. (Because of the Roman rule, the Jews did not have the power to put someone to death, but the officials carefully prepared their case for the upcoming Roman trial.) The Lord refused to answer the questions of Annas concerning His disciples and His teaching, stating that His teaching had been done in public both in the synagogues and the temple. If Annas wanted to know, he could ask those who had heard Him. It was at that point that an official struck Christ in the face.

Before Caiaphas and the Hastily Assembled Sanhedrin

What a beehive of activity Jerusalem must have been! In the early morning hours, Jewish leaders had been summoned from their beds. They hurriedly made their way through the city's dark streets to assemble as the Sanhedrin, a body of seventy judges presided over by the high priest. They felt they needed to deal with the subversive teaching of this itinerant preacher and His band of followers, now that He was in their possession.

After hearing false testimony about the Lord's claims to rebuild the temple in three days, Caiaphas bluntly asked Him if He were the Christ. When He calmly admitted who He was, the high priest tore his clothes in anguish and accused the prisoner of blasphemy. The Jewish officials then proclaimed that He was worthy of death, although this was not a formal sentence. Only the Roman procurator could make such an indictment. At this point, the verdict of guilty simply meant the Jewish governing body now thought it had a case that would secure a death penalty from the Roman authority.

The guards began mocking and beating Jesus, spitting in His face, striking Him with their fists, and slapping Him. They further humiliated the Son of God by blindfolding Him, striking Him, and demanding: "Prophesy! Who is the one who struck You?" (Luke 22:64).

Formal Trial before the Sanhedrin

After such cruel treatment, Jesus was given back to the officers and later led away to await the third part of His Jewish trial. Just after dawn on Friday morning, the Sanhedrin met at the palace of the high priest to briefly question Christ and then ratify the earlier condemnation. After this third Jewish trial, brief as it was, the prisoner was led to the Romans.

The guards began mocking and beating Jesus, spitting in His face, striking Him with their fists, and slapping Him.

In the meantime, while Jesus was being shamefully treated in the palace of the high priest, two men stood nearby. Although all eleven of the apostles in Gethsemane had fled when Jesus was arrested, two of them made their way to the palace. Peter is named in all four of the Gospels. John's account mentions another disciple, probably John. Because this apostle was known to the high priest, he was allowed into the courtyard, but Peter had to wait until his friend spoke to the young girl at the door. She then allowed Peter to enter.

Peter Sifted Like Wheat

Impetuous Peter, the apostle who had a habit of acting before he thought and the one who had only recently claimed that he would never deny the Lord, was the man who was about to crumble as he was sifted as wheat by Satan (Luke 22:31).

The four Gospels tell the story of Peter's denials during these trials, but with different details and not necessarily in the same order. All mention a maid as the first one who voiced her suspicions about this rugged man from Galilee.

At the time of the second denial, Matthew and Mark mention another maid. Luke refers to a man, but John says "they spoke" to Peter. In the account of the third denial, Matthew and Mark characterize the accusers as "they that stood by." Luke uses the term "another man." John mentions "one of the servants of the high priest." There is really no contradiction in the Gospel accounts. In all likelihood several people joined in the talk as Peter was accused each time.

In all likelihood several people joined in the talk as Peter was accused each time.

The first denial happened during the early part of Jesus' trials, shortly after John used his influence to get Peter admitted into the courtyard of the high priest by the young girl. It seems that Peter then was left alone with the Lord's captors as they warmed themselves by a fire in an open court outside the chamber where the trial was taking place before Caiaphas and the hastily assembled Sanhedrin. Remember that it was early spring and Jerusalem was about 2,400 feet up in the mountains.

Fearing discovery of who he was, Peter then moved from the open courtyard to a porch-like part of the palace. When he was again asked if he had been with the prisoner, Peter used stronger language, denying with an oath.

Matthew and Mark place the third denial as "after a little while," but Luke states that it was about an hour later. We are made to wonder what thoughts raced through Peter's mind during the time he was wandering around the palace grounds, hoping no one would recognize him as a follower of the prisoner who was being tried at that very moment. Because no accusations had been made during the past hour, perhaps Peter felt confident to return to the warmth of the fire. This time he was accused of being associated with Christ because of his Galilean accent. At this point, a relative of Malchus, whose ear Peter had cut off with a sword, thought he had seen Peter in the garden just a few hours earlier. Peter must have felt he was in grave danger of arrest himself. To add emphasis to his denial, he began to curse and swear.

Earlier, after the Last Supper, the Master had predicted that Peter would deny Him three times before the cock crowed. Just as the words of denial fell from Peter's lips for the third time, he heard a bone-chilling sound: the crowing of a rooster.

The Look

At this moment Jesus was being taken as a prisoner from one part of the royal palace to another place. Whether or not He heard Peter's denial we do not know, but He certainly could see the rugged fisherman. Luke's words are succinct but so powerful: "And the Lord turned and looked at Peter. And Peter remembered the word of the Lord, how He had said to him, 'Before the rooster crows, you will deny Me three times'" (Luke 22:61). Peter had been caught red-handed in his sin!

How penetrating that gaze must have been when the eyes of the Son of God fell upon His apostle. Undoubtedly it was filled with hurt and mingled with love. That look cut Peter to the heart. "So Peter went out and wept bitterly" (Luke 22:62).

Peter dropped out of the picture for the remainder of Jesus' trials as he groped with his sins in the darkness. However, from that moment, Peter's life was never the same. His heart had been changed.

Before Pilate

Early on that Friday morning, the Jewish officials led the bound Jesus through the streets of Jerusalem to the Praetorium, a magnificent palace that Herod the Great built for himself. The Jews could not enter the building because they would be defiled and could not eat the Passover. Pilate came out to meet them with the question: "What accusation do you bring against this Man?" (John 18:29).

The Jews first claimed their prisoner was an evildoer. (He was accused of blasphemy by the Sanhedrin, but this charge was by no means a criminal offense among the Romans.) Pilate first attempted to save Jesus by telling the Jews to deal with the prisoner according to their law. He wanted to be no part of their verdict. Because the Jewish law was powerless to put Jesus to death, they changed their charge into three accusations, all of which would threaten the Roman Empire: (1) Jesus was misleading their nation, (2) He was refusing to pay taxes to Caesar, and (3) He was claiming to be a king.

When Pilate stepped back into the Praetorium, he questioned Jesus about His kingdom. Meanwhile, the Jews waiting outside were anxious to get their prisoner put to death, hopefully without further trials. We can only imagine the scene as they expectantly awaited Pilate's verdict. When the Roman ruler appeared, for the second time he once again attempted to save Jesus with the simple words, "I find no fault in Him at all" (John 18:38). Pilate did not consider the prisoner to be a threat to Rome.

The crowd became more fierce, saying that Jesus stirred up the people with His teaching, beginning in Galilee and coming all the way to Jerusalem. When Pilate learned that the prisoner was from Galilee, he thought he had found a way to relieve himself of this responsibility. Herod was the tetrarch of Galilee, and he was in town during this time of the Passover. (Neither Herod nor Pilate lived at Jerusalem all the time.) The prisoner was then hurried to Herod's residence.

Before Herod

Herod was greatly pleased when he saw Jesus because he had heard about this man and had wanted to see one of the miracles the people had been talking about. He questioned the prisoner but Jesus answered nothing, even with the chief priests and teachers of the law standing by and vehemently accusing Him. Herod and his soldiers treated the Son of God with contempt as they mocked Him. Dressing Him in a gorgeous robe, Herod returned the Lord to Pilate. Until this time Pilate and Herod had been enemies, but on this day they were made friends. Strange bedfellows!

Before Pilate Again

When Christ was delivered back to Pilate in His newly acquired robe, the Roman ruler called the chief priests and Jewish rulers together. Because neither he nor Herod had found a basis for the charges the Jews had brought against the Lord, Pilate tried once again to spare Jesus by offering to release either Him or Barabbas, who had been thrown into prison for insurrection and murder. According to custom, one prisoner of the people's preference was released at the Passover each year. Probably Pilate thought Jesus would be the less harmful of the two men. Instead, the crowd cried out in loud voices, "Away with this man, and release unto us Barabbas!"

Pilate's wife sent word to her husband: "Have nothing to do with Jesus."

It was at this time that Pilate's wife sent word to her husband that he should have nothing to do with Jesus because of her dream the previous night. Her request undoubtedly had an impact on Pilate because the Romans were greatly influenced by their dreams.

In the meantime, the chief priests and elders worked the crowds outside of Pilate's palace. The next time Pilate appeared before them with his same question regarding their preference of a prisoner to release, they again demanded the release of Barabbas and the death of Christ. Over and over they called out, "Crucify Him!" Pilate continued to try to circumvent their demands.

The Scourging

We tend to read a few simple words from the Scriptures over and over and yet often fail to realize their full meaning: "So then Pilate took Jesus and scourged Him" (John 19:1).

Josephus states that those who were condemned to crucifixion were first scourged, which could be done in two different ways. Sometimes the instruments of torture were thongs or whips made of ropes or leather and loaded with pieces of bone or metal at the ends. At other times the criminal was beaten with rods or twigs.

The Roman custom was to strip the prisoner, tie him to a frame, and then beat him with thongs or rods. Blood usually spurted with the first blow. The Jews had a law that limited the number of blows to forty, but the Romans had no such law and often beat their victims until they bled to death. The blows were so fierce that often not only was the prisoner's back cut but also his face and eyes. Teeth were frequently knocked out.

The Romans often beat their victims until they bled to death.

According to Eusebius, an early church historian, a Roman scourging was described in the following words: "All around were horrified to see them so torn with the scourges that their very own veins were laid bare, and the inner muscles and even their very bowels were exposed." Christ not only suffered severe physical torture, He also was emotionally humiliated. Because He had claimed to be the King of the Jews, the soldiers wove a crown of thorns and placed it on His head in mockery, along with a purple robe denoting royalty. Although, in comparison to scourging, the pain was slight when the crown of thorns was pressed on His head, nevertheless it *did* hurt. The soldiers' mockery, "Hail, King of the Jews!" was heightened by blows on His face.

"Behold the Man!"

Evidently Pilate's plan was to elicit the pity of the Jews by scourging Jesus. When the prisoner was brought out of the building and presented to the jeering crowds, Pilate's words were simple: "Behold, the Man!" Surely they would have pity on the beaten, bloody man standing before them and think that He had been punished enough. Quite to the contrary, the angry Jews once again cried out, "Crucify Him, crucify Him!" Fearing that Pilate was ridiculing them and would do nothing more to Jesus, they brought an additional charge this time. Leviticus 24:16 states that anyone who is guilty of blasphemy is to be put to death. It may not have been mentioned before this time because the Jews knew that Pilate was under no obligation to enforce their laws. Out of desperation they hurled this charge at the broken man standing before them.

Even more afraid, Pilate once again summoned his prisoner into the Praetorium for questioning. Christ was silent. In frustration, Pilate reminded Jesus that he had the power either to release or crucify Him. The Lord reminded the Roman ruler that he could have no authority over Him unless it had been given to him from God and that Caiaphas, who delivered Him, had the greater sin.

Pilate had had enough trouble with the Jews and was aware of what could happen if he made the wrong decision. If Christ were brought before Caesar with charges from the Jews, Pilate could lose his position—or even his life.

"Shall I Crucify Your King?"

It was now approximately six o'clock in the morning. Pilate brought Jesus out and sat on the judgment seat of a place called The Pavement, a large, paved area that was part of the Castle of Antonia. He presented the prisoner to the people with the words, "Behold your King!" Once again the people shouted, "Away with Him, crucify Him!"

In yet another attempt to save the Lord, Pilate asked the people, "Shall I crucify your King?" The chief priests answered, "We have no king but Caesar!" They apparently had forgotten about the promise made to them as descendants of Abraham when they proclaimed Caesar as their king.

In one last attempt to save the Lord's life, Pilate asked the angry crowd what evil Jesus had done. Their demands of crucifixion continued as they shouted even more. Fearing a riot, Pilate gave in to their bloodthirsty demands as he symbolically washed his hands in front of the mob, declaring his innocence of the prisoner's blood. Even though the Jews were aware of the significance of the ceremonial washing of hands (Deuteronomy 21:1–9), in their rage they still demanded the blood of Jesus. After releasing Barabbas to the people, Pilate gave his consent for Jesus to be crucified.

The Tortured Captive

Before Jesus was led to His death of torture, the soldiers took the prisoner back into the Praetorium, where they stripped Him of His blood-splattered clothing, clothed Him with a scarlet robe, jammed a crown of thorns on His head, and placed a useless reed in His right hand. One by one the jeering men knelt before Jesus, took the rod out of His hand, and struck the helpless man on the head, further driving the thorns into His scalp, as they mockingly cried out, "Hail, King of the Jews!" The Scriptures do not reveal how long the Lord was humiliated before the soldiers grew weary of their ridicule and were ready to remove His scarlet robe, put His own clothes back on Him, and lead Him away.

Carrying a cross required a great deal of physical exertion, especially for a man who had been scourged and beaten to the point of death. We cannot imagine how it must have felt to carry the weight of the wood on a back that had already been laid open by whips. It has been estimated that the weight of the entire cross was over three hundred pounds. The crossbar itself (patibulum) weighed between seventy-five and one hundred pounds. Evidently the Lord grew too weak to carry His own cross, because Luke tells us that Simon of Cyrene—a city of North Africa with a large population of Jews—was compelled to carry it for Him.

As Christ, Simon, the two criminals who were also to be put to death, and the soldiers made their way through the streets of Jerusalem, one can only begin to imagine what thoughts must have gone through the Lord's mind. Only a few days earlier, He had been hailed as the Son of David when He rode through the streets of this city on a donkey with the multitudes spreading their garments and tree branches in the way before Him. Now He trudged as a humiliated, tortured captive about to be crucified.

> *He had been hailed as the son of David . . . now He trudged as a humiliated captive about to be crucified.*

The Crucifixion

Suspended between Heaven and Earth

After winding through the streets of Jerusalem, the jeering soldiers led their victims to Golgotha, an execution site on a rocky hill outside the city walls. It was customary to confuse the senses and somewhat deaden the additional pain that was about to be inflicted by offering the men a drink of wine that had been mingled with vinegar and gall (myrrh) to make it bitter. Christ refused.

Roman soldiers held their victim against the cross while they began the process of nailing the outstretched hands and the feet into the wood. We read those words and think we understand, but we really have no concept of the suffering involved.

The finding of nails dating back to the time of the crucifixion reveals they were iron spikes five-to-seven inches long with a square shaft. They were commonly driven through the wrist instead of the palm. We cannot begin to image the victim's horror while flinching from the intense pain of that first blow and realizing that he would also have to endure the torture of having not only his other hand nailed to the wood but also his feet. What terrible agony he must have felt as the cross bearing his body was hoisted in the air and dropped with a dull thud into a hole. There, the victims were left to slowly die as they helplessly writhed in pain from the previous scourging, in addition to the torture of being nailed to the cross. Even lesser pains, such as annoying flies and insects that gathered around their open wounds, must have made the prisoners even more miserable.

The time for the beginning of the crucifixion of Christ is recorded as the third hour—9:00 A.M. As the Lord was suspended between heaven and earth for the next six hours, His eyes witnessed many hurtful scenes.

Jesus could not help but see the Roman soldiers dividing His clothes among themselves and even casting lots for His seamless outer garment.

The people below wagged their heads while they mockingly urged Him to come down from the cross and save Himself.

His ears had to hear the verbal abuse hurled at Him as the people below wagged their heads while they mockingly urged Him to come down from the cross and save Himself, if He were truly the Son of God as He had claimed to be. The Jewish religious officials—chief priests, scribes, and elders—joined in the jeering as they issued the same challenge. The soldiers also mocked Jesus when they offered Him sour wine while urging Him to save Himself. Even one of the criminals hanging beside Jesus hurled abuse at Him as he said, "If You are the Christ, save Yourself and us" (Luke 23:39). Because the other thief realized that he was suffering for his own crimes but Jesus had done nothing worthy of death, his penitent heart found favor with the Lord and he was told that he would be in Paradise with Jesus that very day.

Not everyone was verbally abusing the Lord, however. His eyes must have fallen on His mother, along with several other devoted women, and John the apostle. In spite of all the horror of the cross, Mary still wanted to be near her Son. It would have been difficult to give up a child in any sort of normal death, but to see her own flesh and blood suspended between heaven and earth in such a cruel manner is more than any of us can fathom. It was at this point that Jesus committed her care to His beloved John, who had been brave enough to follow Him to the execution site.

Cries in the Darkness

Between the hours of 9:00 A.M. and noon, the crucifixions on Golgotha proceeded as normal for the Romans. Three men writhed in agony in the midst of verbal abuse from those watching below. But at the sixth hour (12:00 P.M.) the scene began to change.

Noon is normally the time when the sun is overhead at its brightest. On this particular day, however, darkness came over the land at that time and remained for the next three hours. People must have found it necessary to pull out their candles to carry on their normal duties around their homes and in their businesses in Jerusalem. They probably wondered what was happening because they had never before encountered anything like this. The soldiers at the cross undoubtedly had difficulty in taking care of their responsibilities. (We think we have hardships when our electricity is interrupted for thirty minutes. Try to imagine functioning in unexpected darkness for three hours.)

After three hours of groping in the dark, the people witnessing the executions heard an unusual question coming from the lips of the prisoner in the middle as He mustered enough strength to cry out with a loud voice, "My God, My God, why have You forsaken Me?" At that moment the sacrificial Lamb had shouldered the sins of mankind and Jehovah had turned His back on His Son. Some of those standing nearby thought the Lord had called for Elijah. When Jesus said "I thirst!" (John 19:28), someone ran for a sponge filled with vinegar, put it on a reed, and gave Him a drink, saying, "Let Him alone; let us see if Elijah will come to save Him" (Matthew 27:49).

Then the bruised and bleeding Lamb of God proclaimed, "It is finished!" (John 19:30). With a loud voice He cried out, "Father, 'into Your hands I commit My spirit.'" (Luke 23:46).

Earthquake, Open Tombs, and Temple Rending

When Jesus died the people witnessed sights they had never seen before. In the temple, the massive sixty-foot curtain that separated the Holy Place from the Most Holy Place was split from top to bottom, signifying that, under the new law for which Christ had given His life, all believers now would have access to God and the old law was no longer in force.

Not only was the veil torn from top to bottom, but there was also a great earthquake. Rocks split and the tombs broke open. At His resurrection, many holy people being raised to life, went into the city.

When the centurion and others guarding Jesus witnessed these sights, they were terrified and exclaimed, "Truly this Man was the Son of God!" (Mark 15:39).

Because it was Friday and the body of a man on the cross should not be left hanging when the Sabbath arrived at six o'clock that evening, the soldiers broke the legs of the two men crucified with Jesus to hasten their deaths. (Those sentenced to death in this manner had difficulty getting air into their lungs without pushing their bodies up with their legs. Breaking the legs put a stop to their gasps for air and hastened their deaths.) John's account reveals that, after breaking the legs of the other two criminals, they found Jesus already dead. Instead of needlessly breaking His legs, a soldier pierced His side with a spear, causing blood and water to run out.

It was over. The price had been paid.

Christians Are to Remember

The death of Christ is the pivotal point of Christianity. The old law was nailed to the cross (Colossians 2:14), and the blood of Christ became the means of obtaining the forgiveness of sins through baptism.

When Christ instituted the Lord's supper, it was to be a feast of remembrance as His followers would henceforth use unleavened bread and the fruit of the vine to help them recall His body that was nailed to the cross and His blood that was shed for the remission of their sins.

Those first Christians did not serve a dead Christ. Because He arose from the grave on the first day of the week, on that special day they met to remember His painful death (Acts 20:7). It was a feast both of remembering His sacrifice and also His triumph over evil by His resurrection.

Those first Christians did not serve a dead Christ. It was a feast of remembering His sacrifice and His triumph over evil by His resurrection.

Historians record that the early Christians, when facing persecution under Nero, gathered in the catacombs—burial places consisting of small vaults carved out of rock under the streets of Rome—to worship, which included partaking of the Lord's supper. I have been privileged to walk a short distance into the darkness of those narrow, winding paths. With each step I wondered whether or not I would have had enough faith to risk my life to remember the death of the Lord.

Jesus gave His life for the church, His bride. He expects us, as His children, to assemble on the first day of every week to partake of the Lord's supper.

Today Jesus wants us to remember what He sacrificed for us. Instead of hiding in the dark catacombs, we can worship in beautiful, comfortable buildings without fear of death. How does He feel when we allow other things to interfere with the time set aside for recalling His suffering or when we partake of the Lord's supper in a flippant or irreverent manner?

Christ is looking into our hearts today just as He looked into the heart of Peter that night so long ago in the palace of the High Priest: "And the Lord turned and looked at Peter" (Luke 22:61). That gaze prompted Peter to weep bitterly.

May we always be mindful of the deep meaning of this solemn feast of remembrance each time we partake of it.

Questions for Thought

1. In what way was the Passover a schoolmaster to prepare God's people for the significance of the Lord's supper? (Galatians 3:24).

2. Summarize the main events of the days spent in Jerusalem and Bethany before the crucifixion.

3. Why did the apostles have such great difficulty in understanding the spiritual nature of the kingdom?

4. Describe Jesus' object lesson in humility.

5. Compare the Passover to the Lord's supper. In what ways are the two feasts alike? In what ways are they different?

6. Discuss the fact that both the Passover and the Lord's supper were given as memorials before there were any memories.

7. Why do you suppose Jesus did not leave Peter, James, and John with the other eight apostles near the entrance of the garden?

8. Compare the description of Christ in the garden as found in Hebrews 5:7 with the Gospel accounts.

9. Give a medical explanation of Christ's sweating blood in the garden.

10. What do the words "sleeping from sorrow" mean as used in Luke 22:45?

11. By combining the Gospel accounts, relate the events that occurred when the soldiers and Jewish officials arrived in Gethsemane.

12. The first trial was before Annas, the ex-high priest and father-in-law of Caiaphas. Why do you think Jesus was taken here first? How was Christ humiliated?

13. Next, Christ was taken to Caiaphas and a hastily assembled Sanhedrin. What people composed the Sanhedrin and what were their official functions?

14. What physical and emotional pain was inflicted on Jesus when He appeared before the Sanhedrin the first time?

15. Why did the Sanhedrin have to convene again at daylight?

16. Relate the denials of Peter by combining the Gospel accounts.

17. Reflect upon the significance of Luke 22:61–62.

18. What happened the first time Christ appeared before Pilate?

19. Why was Jesus sent to Herod? What happened there?

20. Narrate the events surrounding the second time Christ stood before Pilate.

21. Describe both the physical and the emotional torture of a scourging.

22. Why did Jesus refuse the drink of wine mingled with vinegar and gall?

23. Describe the spikes that were probably used to nail the Lord to the cross.

24. What emotional insults were shouted out to Christ as He hung on the cross?

25. Elaborate on the three-hour darkness that came over the land at noon.

26. What was the significance of the earthquake, the splitting of the veil in the temple, and the resurrection of many holy people?

27. Did God really forsake His Son? Why?

28. Discuss the emblems of the Lord's supper and also the day of the week that it was observed by the early Christians. How do these two factors merge both the death and the resurrection of Jesus?

Notes

Don and Jane, Don's senior banquet, 1955

Old postcard and letter from memorabilia

Wedding: Don McWhorter and Jane Shannon, 1956

D.A.R. and Civitan medalist, Litton High School

4

Remembering: The Feast of Purim

The Feast of Purim is unique because it was not mentioned in the list of feasts God commanded in Exodus 23, Exodus 34, Leviticus 23, Numbers 28, and Deuteronomy 16. Jewish men were required to appear before the Lord for three important festivals:

- *The Passover:* commemorating their deliverance from Egyptian bondage. It was followed immediately by the Feast of Unleavened Bread.
- *Feast of Weeks (Pentecost):* observed fifty days after the Passover and at the beginning of the first fruits of the wheat season.
- *Feast of Tabernacles (Feast of Booths):* given to celebrate the end of the harvest season. During this feast the Israelites were required to live in booths made of boughs of trees to remind them of their lives during the wilderness wanderings.

The Feast of Purim, on the other hand, had no divine directive but instead was initiated by Mordecai during the days of the exile.

> And Mordecai wrote these things and sent letters to all the Jews, near and far, who were in all the provinces of King Ahasuerus, to establish among them that they should celebrate yearly the fourteenth and fifteenth days of the month of Adar, as the days on which the Jews had rest from their enemies, as the month which was turned from sorrow to joy for them, and from mourning to a holiday; that they should make them days of feasting and joy, of sending presents to one another and gifts to the poor . . . that these days should be remembered and kept throughout every generation, every family, every province, and every city, that these days of Purim should not fail to be observed among the Jews, and that the memory of them should not perish among their descendants. (Esther 9:20–28).

Since the time of Esther, faithful Jews have gathered in their synagogues on the prescribed date to hear the entire book of Esther read and once again be reminded of their deliverance from the plot of Haman in the land of Persia so many years ago.

The story, in the setting of an oriental palace with an atmosphere similar to that of *The Arabian Nights*, is filled with drama, suspense, murder, revenge, love, conviction, and trust in God. I invite you to lift the curtain of time with me, step back to the city of Shushan in ancient Persia, and walk the corridors of the palace with Esther and Mordecai.

Historical Setting

The lives of Esther and Mordecai can be better understood if they are considered in their time frame. According to 2 Chronicles 36, the people of Judah were deported from Jerusalem into Babylonian captivity in three stages. The first occurred in 606 B.C. during the days of Jehoiakim when Nebuchadnezzar took this king, Daniel, and other choice people into captivity. In 597 B.C. the pagan ruler captured the succeeding Jewish king (Jehoichin) and others, including Mordecai's family. In 586 B.C. Nebuchadnezzar's army destroyed Jerusalem, after a siege of a year and a half, and took Zedekiah, the brother of Jehoichin, into captivity along with many other Jews.

Unlike the Jews who were carried into Assyrian captivity and then scattered, the Babylonian captives were allowed to settle in communities of their own and lead somewhat normal lives.

Eventually the Babylonian Empire was toppled by the Persians under Cyrus, who was favorable to the Jewish race. In 538 B.C. he issued an edict, allowing God's people to return to their native land. In 536 B.C.—seventy years after the first deportation in 606 B.C.—nearly fifty thousand Jews made the long trip back to Jerusalem, where they withstood the pressures from their adversaries, rebuilt the altar, resumed animal sacrifices, and eventually rebuilt the temple.

While the Jews were struggling to restore the worship of Jehovah in a devastated city without walls for protection, other fascinating events were taking place a thousand miles away in the Persian city of Shushan, the home of many captive Jews who had chosen to remain in the land of their captivity rather than return to their homeland.

The Babylonian captives were allowed to settle in communities of their own and lead somewhat normal lives.

The events of the book of Esther transpired between the happenings of the sixth chapter of Ezra (the dedication of the temple) and those of the seventh chapter (the arrival of Ezra the scribe to teach the law of God).

The heroic actions of two Jewish cousins in a foreign land were instrumental in restoring the dignity of the Jewish people and ultimately paved the way for Ezra and Nehemiah to return for their important work of teaching the people and rebuilding the walls of Jerusalem.

A Royal Feast

Ahasuerus (Xerxes), who succeeded his father (Darius the Great) as ruler of the vast Persian Empire, lived in a magnificent palace in Shushan in an exotic setting of wealth and splendor. The Persian Empire extended from India to Ethiopia. Three years into his reign, after hosting a six-month festival for the chief men of his kingdom's 127 provinces (probably to display his wealth as well as to seek the advice of his statesmen and their support for his upcoming expedition against the Greeks), the powerful ruler climaxed the extravaganza by hosting a one-week festival for all the people, both great and small, at the palace of Shushan.

Men and women did not attend such public occasions together. Queen Vashti hosted a separate feast for the women.

Excavations attest to the magnificence of this residence of the Persian kings. Because the room in the palace was not large enough for so many guests, the king selected the court of the garden within the palace walls as the site for this seven-day feast. The space was nearly 350 feet long by 250 feet wide, with a square of 145 feet taken out of it for the central building. The area exceeded 60,000 square feet.

Esther 1:6–7 gives a description of the opulence of this palace setting: elaborate hangings fastened to silver rings and pillars of marble with cords of fine linen and purple; beds of gold and silver, where the guests reclined as they ate; a pavement of red, blue, white, and black marble; and drinking vessels of gold, each one different from the others.

Because men and women did not attend such public occasions together, Queen Vashti hosted a feast for the women in another part of the royal palace—probably the harem—during the time of the men's seven-day revelry.

Humiliation Followed Revelry

After seven continuous days of unlimited drinking, naturally the king's heart was merry with wine—a polite way of saying that he and the other men were drunk. For seven days he had displayed his wealth and power, but one of his prized possessions had not yet been seen: his beautiful wife! (Vashti means "beautiful.") Saving the best for last, he ordered his seven chamberlains (eunuchs) to bring Vashti, wearing her royal crown, to appear before his guests.

The Scriptures are silent regarding what Vashti's attire (or lack of it) would be as she was expected to parade before the gawking eyes of the king's drunkened guests. The men would not be able to see her beauty if she appeared with her veil, so we may safely surmise that Ahasuerus expected at least that part of clothing to be removed. (In that culture it was shameful for a woman to appear unveiled before any man except her husband.) In all likelihood, Vashti was expected to remove most of her clothes when she appeared before the lustfully gazing eyes of the drunk men.

We may safely suppose that Vashti was not a worshiper of Jehovah. Although supposedly a pagan, she highly regarded modesty and had the conviction to make a stand for her belief. We can only imagine the look on the face of Ahasuerus when his seven chamberlains returned with the queen's answer: "No!"

Ahasuerus was furious when he was humiliated by his wife's refusal to appear before his guests. He sought the council of his wise men, who advised him to depose Vashti from her royal position. A decree proclaiming the king's action was spread throughout the vast empire lest the other women in the kingdom should follow her example of failing to give honor to their husbands.

The Search for a New Queen

The years following the deposition of Vashti were charged with emotions for King Ahasuerus (Xerxes). Not only had his queen humiliated him but his troops also met defeat in the military campaign against Greece.

Evidently the king's counselors thought it would help him forget Vashti and lift his morale if he furnished his harem with beautiful new women and selected a new queen. He agreed to their proposal. Consequently, officers in all 127 provinces were instructed to find the most beautiful virgins in Persia. The young women were to be taken to the harem in his palace in Shushan for a year of purification—which included the beauty treatment of the day with oils and perfumes and also gave ample time for a hidden pregnancy to become evident—before they were brought before Ahasuerus for his final selection of a new queen.

Her Persian name, Esther, means "star." Her Jewish name, Hadassah, means "a myrtle."

One of the young virgins selected was Hadassah. (Esther became her Persian name). Earlier, when Esther's parents died in the land of their captivity, Mordecai, her uncle's son, had adopted her and became a father figure to her. (Were the deaths of her parents natural or violent? The Scriptures are silent.) *Esther*, her Persian name when she became the queen means "star." *Hadassah*, her Jewish name, means "a myrtle." The myrtle was a plant of sweet-scented and luxuriant beauty. Esther's beauty made her a natural candidate for this national Persian beauty contest.

The young women, after a year of purification in the house of the virgins, went to the king one at a time in the evening when they were called and returned to the harem the next morning. From that time on, they left the house of the virgins and entered the house of the concubines, where they were to live for the rest of their lives, never being allowed to marry anyone else and only seeing the king when he called for them. The one who would be selected as the queen would have her own private residence in the harem.

Above All Women

When Esther's time to go to the king arrived, she was not interested in elaborate clothes or jewels but instead relied on the advice of the chief eunuch regarding what was appropriate. "And Esther obtained favor in the sight of all who saw her" (Esther 2:15). Her natural beauty, coupled with her inner attractiveness, made her irresistible to Ahasuerus and she was made his queen. In celebration of the occasion, the king made a great feast for the woman he loved "more than all the other women" (Esther 2:17). Esther kept her heritage to herself as Mordecai had instructed her.

Shortly after Esther became queen, Mordecai, who held the position of a keeper at the king's gate, discovered an assassination plot by two of Ahasuerus' chamberlains, who guarded the entrance to his sleeping quarters. He passed the information along to the queen. In turn, she told the king; the two men were killed. Although nothing was done to reward Mordecai at that time, his brave deed was entered into the king's official chronicles.

Haman's Revenge

Later Haman, a Persian, was promoted to the position of prime minister. Although others bowed before the man who was now second to the king and gave him reverence, Mordecai adamantly refused. The king's servants questioned Mordecai about his actions, but he refused to listen to them. Knowing that he was a Jew, they told Haman about Mordecai's defiant stand. Haman was enraged!

It is altogether possible that Mordecai's extreme dislike of Haman can be traced back to Haman's ancestry. He is referred to as "Haman, the son of Hammedatha the Agagite" in Esther 3:1. God had told King Saul to kill King Agag when he attacked Amalek. Instead of obeying God, Saul spared this man, along with the best of the animals (supposedly for sacrifices.) When Samuel learned of King Saul's disobedience, the prophet cut Agag into pieces (1 Samuel 15:33).

The Amalekites were the first enemies to attack the Israelites after their exodus from Egypt. Exodus 17:8–16 relates the incident of Aaron and Hur holding up of the hands of Moses while Joshua fought the Amalekites. In 1 Samuel 30 may be found the story of David's defeat of these bitter enemies after they had destroyed Ziklag and had carried away all the women as captives. Understandably, there had been bad blood between the Amalekites and the Israelites for many, many years.

Haman's Challenge—Exterminate the Race!

Not being content to simply have Mordecai killed alone, Haman sought more vengeance. He would have all the Jews in the Persian Empire destroyed! Because of his position of authority, he probably could have had one man executed without much trouble. But having an entire race exterminated would require the king's approval.

First, a time would have to be set. Because the Persians were a superstitious people, Haman and his friends cast lots ("pur"), similar to rolling dice, in the first month of the year to find the most auspicious time for this wicked massacre. By this means they determined that the date would be eleven months in the future—the thirteenth day of the twelfth month (Adar), which would correspond with our February–March.

Second, Haman realized that his scheme would be expensive. When the traitor made his requests known, he made his plan more palatable by offering a staggering sum of money to the king, whose treasury had been severely depleted by his campaign against Greece. (The Scriptures do not indicate whether Haman intended to donate the money himself or if he planned to use Jewish properties that would be seized in the massacre.) The justification for the annihilation of the Jews was based upon a half-truth (an accusation that their laws were different and they did not keep the king's laws).

Haman was successful in convincing Ahasuerus, and the king gave him his signet ring to authorize the written decree. The evil revenge had been set in motion.

Not being content to simply have Mordecai killed alone, Haman sought more vengeance. He'd kill all the Jews!

When Mordecai learned of the decree, he expressed his sorrow by putting on sackcloth (rough and made of hair) and ashes, in addition to crying with a loud and bitter voice. As the Jews learned of their fate, they mourned in the same manner.

Mordecai's Charge to Esther

When Esther's maids told her about Mordecai's plight, she sent clothes, which he refused to wear. Then she sent one of her servants to find out why Mordecai was acting in such a manner. Mordecai responded by forwarding a copy of the decree to Esther with the charge that she should go before the king with a supplication for her people.

What a heart-wrenching time that must have been for Esther. She sent word to Mordecai that anyone—man or woman—who came into the presence of the king without his special invitation could be put to death. To compound her plight, the queen stated that she had not been invited into the presence of the king in thirty days!

Mordecai reminded Esther that, although she had not yet revealed her identity, her life was at stake just as much as that of any other Jew. *All* would be destroyed. Then Mordecai sent those often-quoted words back to his adopted daughter: "Who knows whether you have come to the kingdom for such a time as this?" (Esther 4:14).

Gathering courage for the course that Esther knew she must take, she sent word to Mordecai to gather all the Jews in Shushan for a three-day fast. During that time she and her maidens would do the same. At the end of that period she would take her petition to the king. Her final words to Mordecai were, "If I perish, I perish!" (Esther 4:16).

Esther Dares to Take Action

With the realization that appearing uninvited before the king could very easily result in death, Esther adorned herself with her royal apparel, summoned her courage, and stepped into the inner court of the palace in view of Ahasuerus as he was sitting on his regal throne. We cannot begin to imagine what her emotions must have been at that moment. Would she be banished to death for daring to come uninvited into the king's presence or would he extend his golden scepter to her? Even if he permitted her to talk with him, could she be successful in persuading him to save the Jews from extinction in the Persian Empire?

Ahasuerus reacted favorably to the presence of Esther that day. Not only did he extend his golden scepter to her but he also asked about her request, promising her as much as half the kingdom.

Feed Them First

Esther was wise. Rather than laying her request at the king's feet at that moment, she delayed, simply asking him to attend a banquet later that day with Haman.

During the course of that meal, the king once more asked his queen what she desired. Again she postponed her answer, asking him, along with Haman, to come to a second banquet the next day. She promised that she would make her petition known at that time.

Haman was elated over being included with the king to Esther's special banquets. However, as he passed by Mordecai at the gate, he once again felt the humiliation of Mordecai's refusal to bow down to him. As soon as he reached home, he called for his wife and his friends and tried to build up his shattered ego by reminding them of all his glories, climaxing his achievements with the news that only he had been invited to these royal banquets. However, his countenance must have changed as he mused that all these glories were meaningless as long as Mordecai refused to bow before him.

All these glories were meaningless as long as Mordecai refused to bow before Haman.

Zeresh (Haman's wife) and his friends had a simple solution to his problem. If Mordecai seemed to be a nuisance, just have a seventy-five foot gallows built, ask the king to have Mordecai killed, and then go on to the banquet the next day with a merry heart. Haman liked the plan and had the gallows constructed immediately.

The International Standard Bible Encyclopedia (Vol. IV, p. 2505) states that the word *gallows* in the modern sense was unknown to the ancients. "Where the word occurs in Esther . . . it probably refers to a beam or pole on which the body was impaled and then elevated to a height of 50 cubits as an object of warning to the people."

The Adversary Revealed

Not too far away that night, the king also had a problem—insomnia. Perhaps he reasoned that listening to the royal chronicles of the events of the kingdom would produce drowsiness. When the account of Mordecai's foiling of an assassination attempt on the king's life was read to him, he inquired whether or not Mordecai had ever been honored for this service. At this moment in the early morning hours, Haman, who had come to get permission to hang Mordecai, appeared in the court just outside the king's bedchamber. After Ahasuerus gave his permission for Haman to come into his presence, the king asked him what he would suggest for someone who should be honored. Haman, believing that he himself was the one whom the king had in mind, suggested that the man to be honored should be arrayed in royal apparel, placed on the king's own horse, and led by a prince through the streets as he proclaimed the virtues of the honored man. Imagine the expression on Haman's face as he himself led the man whom he hated in royal robes through the town on horseback a short while later!

"The adversary and enemy is this wicked Haman!"

Just as Haman reached home after his humiliating experience, the king's chamberlains arrived to take him to Esther's second banquet. During that meal the king again asked Esther to make her request. This time she boldly asked him to preserve her people from annihilation. When he asked her who would presume to take such action, Esther stated simply, "The adversary and enemy is this wicked Haman!" (Esther 7:6).

Ahasuerus was so angry that he had to step out into the garden to regain his composure. In the meantime Haman, the whimpering coward, began pleading for his life as he fell across Esther's couch. When the king again entered the room, he viewed Haman's position as an assault on the queen and ordered him hanged on the gallows he had previously prepared for Mordecai. After Esther revealed her relationship to Mordecai, Ahasuerus gave his signet ring and Haman's position in the kingdom to her cousin and foster father.

Save My People!

Once again Esther fell at the feet of the king, begging for a decree to reverse the destruction of the Jews. Although the first decree could not be rescinded, the second one allowed the Jews to protect their lives and property on the day originally appointed for their destruction, the thirteenth of Adar. When that day finally arrived, over 75,000 enemies of the Jews were killed throughout the empire, with the rulers assisting the Jews. Five hundred people were killed in the palace in addition to the ten sons of Haman.

The king then asked Esther if she had any further requests. She asked that Haman's ten dead sons be hanged on gallows for all to see, plus an additional purging of the enemies of the Jews in Shushan the next day, which resulted in the deaths of three hundred more enemies.

Following this victory, the Jews gathered in Shushan to celebrate. Because lots (pur) had been cast to select the day of slaughter, the feast of celebration was called the Feast of Purim. For centuries the Jews have continued to celebrate God's deliverance through the actions of Esther and Mordecai in this annual feast.

A Memory to Pass on

Davis Dictionary of the Bible (p. 672) sheds light on the manner in which Jews have celebrated their deliverance from a massacre by their Persian enemies.

The name of the feast was derived from the *pur,* or lot, that Haman cast to find a day that would be the most auspicious for the proposed annihilation of the Jews—the thirteenth day of the twelfth month (Adar), which would correspond to our February–March. Purim has enjoyed popularity among the Jews from the time it was instituted.

On the thirteenth day of Adar the people fast. In the evening, the beginning of the fourteenth day, the Jews assemble for an evening service during which time the scroll (Megillah) of Esther is read aloud. *Davis Dictionary of the Bible* (p. 672) gives the following description of the interaction of the people with the reading of the book of Esther:

> When the name of Haman is reached, the congregation cries out, "Let his name be blotted out," or "The name of the wicked shall rot," while the youthful worshipers spring rattles. The names of Haman's sons are all read in a breath, to indicate that they were hanged simultaneously.

The next morning, the fourteenth day of Adar, the people again assemble in the synagogue to finish the formal religious exercises and then devote the rest of the day to rejoicing and in sending portions of food to one another as well as in the giving of gifts to the poor by the wealthy.

Margaret Hess in her book, *Esther: Courage in Crisis* [(Wheaton, IL: Victor Books, 1980), p. 140] makes the following comments about the observance of Purim:

> When Esther is read in the synagogue, the service is not solemn and quiet like most Jewish services. Whenever the reader mentions Haman's name, the audience stamps its feet and makes noises to boo Haman. Historically, celebrants have concocted all kinds of noisemakers. They would shake stones in metal or whirl wooden noise-makers to make a whining or a clacking sound. Sometimes, they wrote the name of Haman on the soles of their shoes, and then stamped to rub it out. Children entered into the noisemaking with special gusto.

The same author goes on to say that a visitor to Tel Aviv at the time of the Feast of Purim would witness parades, banners, feasts, parties, dancing in the streets and Purim plays. Not only is the book of Esther read in the synagogues, it is also broadcast by loudspeakers to people in the streets. It is a time for unrestrained merrymaking.

Ms. Hess also adds (p. 141) that the book of Esther is read in Jewish synagogues around the world. Although it is not a holy day, families gather. Shops in Jewish neighborhoods carry special Purim pastries, including the *hamantaschen* (three-cornered pastries) that are supposed to represent Haman's hat or the three people at Esther's banquet. A complete celebration of Purim includes fasting the day before, remembering Esther's fast before she appealed to the king.

Although the Feast of Purim was not divinely commanded, it has been observed for centuries because God's providence was important to His people, and they wanted to remember. A permanent record was made at the time of the first observance so the memories could be passed on to future generations.

What a perfect example of the power of written words in preserving memories!

Questions for Thought

1. Discuss the significance of the three major Jewish feasts as described in Leviticus 23.

2. The Feast of Purim, although not divinely commanded, has remained popular to the Jewish people through the centuries. Why do you think it was so important?

3. Who initiated the observance of this feast? (Esther 9:20–28).

4. How was the treatment of the Jews who were carried into Assyrian captivity different from those taken to Babylon?

5. When Cyrus issued the decree for the Jews to be allowed to return to their native land, fewer than fifty thousand made the journey. Why do you suppose all the Jews did not take advantage of this opportunity to go home?

6. The events in the book of Esther take place in the time period between the sixth and seventh chapters of Ezra. List the major events in the first six chapters of Ezra to get a time frame of what happened immediately before the events in the book of Esther.

7. Describe the feast that Ahasuerus hosted for his guests in the palace garden. Do you think his request for Vashti was unreasonable? What do you think it involved? Describe what his feelings must have been when the queen refused.

8. Why did it take a year to select a new queen? Do some research on life in a harem?

9. Do you think that Esther's spending a night with the king before they were married was justified in God's sight? What about Solomon and David and their many wives and concubines?

10. What was Haman's position in the government of Persia? Why did Mordecai refuse to bow down before this man? What was Haman's plan for revenge?

11. Try to step into Esther's shoes as she appeared before the king uninvited. How many days had it been since she had been asked to enter his presence? What could have been the outcome? Why did she want Haman to be present at the dinner?

12. Narrate the events that transpired from the time Haman knew he had been invited to a special dinner to the time he was carried away to the gallows.

13. Describe the gallows in ancient times.

14. What was done to counterattack the first decree of the annihilation of the Jews?

15. Discuss Esther's part in this second decree and also in the second day of killings in Shushan. Was she bloodthirsty?

16. Read Esther 9:16–32 and discuss the original keeping of the Feast of Purim.

17. Describe the Feast of Purim as it is observed today.

18. Why has the memory of Purim been so important to the Jews?

Jane debating at Lipscomb

CLARA ARMSTRONG AND JANE SHANNON
Senior Women's Division

Jane's mother observes Greg aiming his Christmas BB gun, 1972

ARMY AIR FORCES
CHANUTE FIELD, ILLINOIS

Most Representative Students

BENNY NELMS, Freshman; JANE SHANNON, Sophomore; and HOPE CAMP, Junior

Jane chosen as one of most representative students, Lipscomb

Forensic Squad

Row: Maxine Smith, Norma Riggs, Charles Trevathan, James
Row: Jess Hall, Don McWhorter, Vice-President; Wayne Tincher, C
oniel; Wilma Campbell, Jane Shannon, Secretary-Treasurer. Third Row
Coach: Phillip Morrison, President: Marlin Connelly, Paul Rogers, Philip Slate

Forensic Squad at David Lipscomb
(Jane, 2nd row far right)

Memory 101: The Human Brain

Creation

The first two chapters of Genesis relate the details of the creation of the earth and its inhabitants. Man cannot begin to imagine the breathtaking beauty of the pristine world as it existed by the end of the fifth day of creation. Lush vegetation covered the land. During the day the brightness of the sun highlighted the ripples in the streams and the waves of the sea. The shadows of the night were accented by the beauty of the moon and the twinkling of the stars. The waters teemed with all manner of marine life, and the skies were filled with the fowls of the air. God saw that it was good.

On the sixth day the Almighty created all the animals that inhabit the dry ground. Again everything was good. But one thing was lacking. From the dust of the ground, He created the first man in His own image. Taking one of Adam's ribs, God formed Eve.

Far from the false theory of evolution, the Scriptures do not teach that man evolved from lower life. Only Adam and Eve were made in the image of God and they were given dominion over the fish of the sea, the fowls of the air, and all animals on the earth.

> Then God said, "Let Us make man in Our image, according to Our likeness; let them have dominion over the fish of the sea, over the birds of the air, and over the cattle, over all the earth and over every creeping thing that creeps on the earth." So God created man in His own image; in the image of God He created him; male and female He created them (Genesis 1:26–27).

A Distinguishing Trait

From the very beginning, human beings differed from lower forms of life because they were made in the image of God. Memory is one of the distinguishing traits of mankind.

Some lower forms of life have the ability to return to habitats where they have lived in previous times. For example, a salmon will swim upstream to spawn at the very place where it was hatched. Certain kinds of butterflies will migrate to a previous place where they had lived. The same is true of some birds. However, these creatures are acting upon a God-given instinct rather than memory.

In addition to good *instincts,* some animals seem to have good *memories.* Periodically a newspaper article will feature the story of a displaced dog or cat that has traveled many miles—sometimes more than a hundred—to the home of its owner. Elephants are known for their good memories, walking long distances during a drought to a waterhole that had supplied water in a previous dry spell.

Humans differ from lower forms of life because they are made in the image of God.

The brains of human beings are far more complex than those of mere animals, because they are made in the image of God. Man has the ability to reason and reach conclusions. For example, Eve did not disobey

God's instructions not to eat of the fruit of the tree of the know-ledge of good and evil because she could not remember what He had said. She remembered His instructions all too well (Genesis 3:2–3). Instead, the serpent beguiled Eve (Genesis 3:13).

Throughout the pages of the Bible we find stories of people who remembered what God had told them to do but chose instead to do their own will. Consider, for example, the disobedience of Lot's wife in looking back over her hometown as they were fleeing (Genesis 19:17–26). The Scriptures do not record a memory loss; instead, she chose to disobey.

A Scientific Study

In the first section of this study, we focused upon the importance of memory in the Scriptures. In addition to that general survey, we devoted much time to examining three important feasts that centered around remembering some special events: the Passover, the Lord's supper, and the Feast of Purim. In this chapter—based upon some basic psychological material—we are going to look at a few primary principles concerning memory and how it works. Because it is a fundamental study, we have selected the title "Memory 101: The Human Brain." We need to understand some elementary facts about our memories before we consider ways to redeem the gold in the earlier events of our lives, as well as learn ways to make the days yet to come a priceless heritage to be treasured. I invite you to roll up your sleeves and join me in an academic study of memories as they relate to the human brain.

The Amazing Power of the Brain

Studies have shown that the human nervous system is composed of billions of nerve cells (neurons), arranged in systems and pathways; each one connects to the others in thousands of different ways. Concentrations of neurons are found in the spinal cord, the brain stem, and the brain. This amazing part of our bodies has been compared to a network of telephone switchboards for all the major cities, constantly connecting the thousand of calls—some local and some long distance—that are transmitted every second. These cells are working all the time, day and night, collecting information, storing it, using it to draw conclusions as well as to solve problems and create feelings and desires.

This amazing part of our bodies has been compared to a network of telephone switchboards for all major cities.

When we encounter a new situation, the brain sorts through all its memory files for a similar situation in order to deal with the new one. For example, consider the challenge of driving a car in Great Britain. If you had flown to London and rented a car to explore the countryside, you would automatically use your previous knowledge of driving skills. You would know how to start the engine and apply the brakes to stop the vehicle. That much would be automatic and you would rely solely on your subconscious mind to get the car on the road. But then there would be a problem. Your automatic thinking had never been programmed to drive on the left side of the road. Your brain consciously took charge of the situation until your subconscious mind gradually took over the wheel. All seemingly went well until you encountered an emergency situation. Suppose someone walked in front of your car and you had to swerve to avoid hitting the person. Your automatic response would be to steer your car to the right because stress had caused you to revert to the original knowledge stored in the memory. Whenever your mind finds itself in an unfamiliar situation, it automatically goes through your memory files to find a similar incident to use as a basis for the appropriate action to take. Then that solution is added to your basic core of knowledge for future use.

Years later, when you reflect upon any memory, you will find that the factual happenings were stored with their accompanying emotional memories. Think of something very special that happened in your life. An appropriate trigger can elicit the smells, the tastes of food, the warmth of hugs or, conversely, the fear and panic of a situation. The emotions are locked into the factual happening. As a matter of fact, they are inseparably entwined with the event and, good or bad, forever color your perception of the incident.

Three Primary Kinds of Memory

Scholars who deal with the working of the mind recognize three basic *kinds* of memory: episodic memory, somatic data, and procedural memory.

Episodic Memory

This memory involves some *event* that you've experienced. Think of happenings in your lifetime—a happy day in your childhood, an unpleasant experience when you were young, your graduation from high school or college, your wedding, your first day on your new job, the birth of your children, or any other happening in your life.

Somatic Data

All the bits of information you've stored in your mind—the general knowledge you've acquired through the years—is somatic data. The storehouse of tidbits required to win a game of Trivial Pursuit is a good example of this kind of knowledge. It doesn't matter whether or not the information is important to your life. It's just there in your brain. Some people are masters of being able to retain millions of isolated facts for long periods of time. Others are not.

Procedural Memory

This is a recollection of all the tasks you have learned *how* to do—drive a car, type, skate, use a lawn mower, play a piano, ride a bicycle, play baseball, shoot a gun, or hit a golf ball. These skills of *how to do something* have been practiced until they have become almost an automatic reflex that you perform intuitively. The repetition of correct movements has been so ingrained in your mind that you do them without any conscious effort.

By way of summary, you remember episodes or happenings from your life (episodic memory), bits and pieces of information (somatic data), and how to perform routine tasks (procedural memory). All are stored in your brain's memory.

Three Stages of Memory

Sensory Holding

This is the part of the brain that receives raw data from the outside world. Through the avenues of sight, taste, smell, touch or hearing, the brain receives information, which it holds for a very short period of time until it can be passed on to short-term memory.

Short-term Memory

Short-term memory receives the raw data from the holding compartments of the five senses. This stage of our memory is at work for a very short time after receiving new information. Throughout any twenty-four-hour period, the short-term memory absorbs thousands of sights, smells, tastes, touches, and sounds from the sensory holding. Most of them are disregarded. Meaningful information is transferred to short-term memory. The other impulses that the short-term memory receives are usually forgotten. Short-term memory keeps the pertinent facts in mind only as long as needed to get the task done, and then normally those memories fade completely. For example, as long as we are staying at a motel, we usually remember our room number fairly well. A week later, that number has vanished from the mind. It served a purpose for a time, but it was not important enough to become a part of our long-term memory.

To give another example, through our ears our *sensory holding* may receive a phone number when we dial information. After repeating the ten-digit number to ourselves, we may think we can remember it. However, usually we fail miserably if we don't write the numbers on a piece of paper because seven unrelated numbers are normally the limit the short-term memory can hold at a time. The holding capacity of short-term memory is called the *memory span*. Have you ever entered a room to get something only to go blank when you stepped into the room? You probably got side-tracked when you set out on your mission, and your intention flew out the window.

Once memories have been transferred to long-term memory, they continue to be reworked.

Long-Term Memory

Long-term memory receives messages from the short-term memory as they pass through the "gatekeeper of memory." One reason a particular message entered the gate of long-term memory could have been because there was some trait in that message that received our undivided attention and caused us to focus intently on it. Or perhaps through association with existing memories, a new linkage or path in the brain was built.

For example, through repetition and intense focusing, phone numbers can be transferred to long-term memory until their recall becomes automatic. Once memories have been transferred to the long-term memory, they are never stored and stagnant but continue to be reworked below the conscious level. More will be said about long-term memories later.

Saving Memories

The three processes in the saving of memories are encoding, storage, and retrieval.

Encoding

This process is simply a translation of the impulses received through the external senses to the internal part of the brain, sent first to short-term memory.

✳ *Synapses* is the term applied to the connections between the nerves. A tiny impulse—electrical and chemical—crosses the synapse, forming a nerve linkage. When an impulse crosses a synapse, a path has been formed, making future crossings easier. Habits are made when thoughts and actions have crossed this path so often that they have become ingrained.

For example, the more selections that musicians memorize, the easier it becomes for them to learn additional musical scores. Public speakers who become accustomed to committing their messages to memory find new memorization even easier as more and more synapses are formed in their brains.

✳ *Sifting* takes place in the short-term memory during the encoding process. After the brain encodes stimuli received from the external senses, it then begins sifting through the information for anything interesting and meaningful and discards the rest.

For example, through the sense of our eyes we may look at a beautiful painting in an art gallery. Images from the work of art pass over synapses into our short-term memory (encoding). At that point the short-term memory begins *sifting* through the messages it is receiving for something significant about those impulses. Non-meaningful impulses are eventually discarded as the rest of the painting fades in our memories. As the brain sifts, it usually also *sorts* the information according to previously formed patterns and categories, making it easier to remember. For example, we can remember more easily the name of a person to whom we've just been introduced if we can associate that name with something that is already meaningful in our lives. As mentioned earlier, the holding capacity of short-term memory is called *memory span*. Most people's memory span is only about seven unrelated items.

> *Most people's memory span is only about seven unrelated items.*

Storage

Not every stimulus that enters the brain is saved. Unless the stimulus is meaningful to us in some way, it is usually forgotten. At times it can be meaningful, but something may divert our attention, and that stimulus is forgotten before it ever reaches the long-term memory. The erasing of memories before they have time to reach the long-term memory is called *decay*.

How much of a stimulus is passed from short-term to long-term memory depends upon several factors. One pertains to the *filter of our emotions and our interest* at the time of the happening. If our *emotions* at that time were happy, the long-term memory will sift out any unpleasant experience associated with the happening and retain only the good ones. Conversely, if our emotions were characterized by sadness, the long-term memory probably discarded some positive, happy memories and stored only the negative ones.

Our *interest* at the time of the event is also instrumental in whether or not the long-term memory retains all the details. We tend to remember what interests us and forget other parts of that happening. For example, an avid football fan may remember scores, plays, and players of previous games to an extent that is amazing to those with little interest in the sport.

Another filter in the storage of memories is *distortion*. The brain does not always accurately store an event in its long-term memory. Sometimes it is distorted by our cultures, our backgrounds, our beliefs, or other factors that influence our outlook on life. In a sense, all serve as filters. For example, some of our memories may be distorted by our parents' descriptions of an event, which may not always accurately portray what actually happened. Even though we were a part of the making of that memory and saw it through a child's eyes, we may have heard those distorted stories from our parents' point of view often enough that they became the truth to us.

Denial serves as a factor in what the long-term memory stores from the information it receives. Memories are not erased, but sometimes events and emotions are so painful that we simply cannot cope with their remembrance at the present time, so we build a protective wall around them by pretending they do not exist. However, those memories are still there, buried deeply under the surface.

Some of our memories may be distorted by our parents' descriptions of an event.

Erosion is yet another factor in what memories are kept in storage. Brain cells die because of age and also from misuse. Actively using our brains, rehearsing information over and over, and repeating it often can prevent much erosion.

Retrieval

Both encoding and storage are vital in using long-term memories, but of equal importance is the *retrieval* of stored information. Long-term memory is never really lost. Instead, the inability to recall may lie in our retrieval system.

Recognition is vital in the retrieval of memories. We meet thousands of people in a lifetime, and their faces are stored in our long-term memories. For example, we may run into a person whom we haven't seen for several years. Although we may not be able to call her name, usually we will recognize her face as one that is familiar.

Recall is another factor in the retrieval of memories. Much as a dog retrieves a ball, the brain retrieves stored information when asked. During school days, we usually crammed information into our brains while studying for a test and then hoped we could recall that data when presented with test questions by the teacher.

A *trigger* is any stimulus that brings a memory out of storage. In the example mentioned in the previous paragraph, test questions served as triggers to retrieve the stored information from the student's brain. Our senses are of equal importance in retrieving information. Sights, smells, sounds, touches, and tastes can bring a flood of memories as they trigger the retrieval of something we have not thought about in years. All along, it had been there, embedded in the long-term memory as it had waited for some trigger to cause it to spring to life again. For example, the smell of homemade yeast rolls may conjure a scene of your family gathered around the dinner table many years ago. The memory had always been there; it simply needed a trigger to bring it to the surface.

Jehovah was very wise in using many of the senses of His people in the observance of the Passover. Not only did they hear the story of their deliverance retold each year but they also first-handedly experienced the sights, the textures, the smells, and the tastes of the food prepared for that first Passover meal so long ago in the land of bondage.

For a number of years I have kept a journal of significant happenings in my life. Although I may not have thought about any of the events in a number of years, reading those words always triggers many vivid memories. Not only does the event come back to life but also the accompanying smells, the touches, and the sounds. Quite often one memory will trigger another one in the same general category.

Memories Reflect Who We Are

In the long-term section of the brain, memories are constantly flowing, much like an underground river that has been running since early childhood. For better or for worse, our childhood memories shape the self-image of the person we are today. In fact, our personalities are fairly well formed even before we are old enough to go to school. An examination of our early memories can help us understand our temperaments, our strengths, and our weaknesses.

During a child's early years, he accepts the messages he receives without questioning, because he does not have the maturity to discern truth from error. If his parents called him stupid, he generally accepted that evaluation as being right because of his immaturity. If the adults around him never praised his accomplishments nor seemed pleased with him, he grew up thinking he was worthless. If he was constantly told he was ugly, then that became his evaluation of himself. On the other hand, fortunate is the youngster whose parents looked for his good points and praised him for them. That child developed a healthy concept of himself as a person with some weaknesses (because he was only human) but whose strengths outweighed his negative traits. As a result, he grew up believing he was a person of worth who had something to contribute to the world.

Becoming Our Programming

We generally live up to whatever has been programmed into our subconscious minds because those early messages tend to become prophetic. We develop into the person who has been molded during those formative years unless we can recognize those negative evaluations as false and do something to change them.

Acting either adversely or constructively on earliest memories largely determines the person we are today. For example, a child growing up in a home where procrastination was the norm usually takes one of two turns. Either he will accept putting things off and being tardy as a way of life or else he will rebel and insist that things be done ahead of schedule. The same is true of neatness and clutter. If his earliest memories are of a home where there was a place for everything and everything was in its place, he may well adopt that philosophy as his own way of life. Or, orderliness may have been so revolting to him that he chooses to live a more relaxed, cluttered life. (By the way, have you ever noticed that a neatnic rarely ever marries another neatnic? Isn't it strange that a punctual person usually winds up marrying someone who is never on time?)

Distorted Memories

As mentioned earlier, not every memory is accurate; some are distorted. Mature adults should be able to look back on their early memories and discern which ones are true and which are distorted.

The more often they retell the event, the more factual the embellishments become.

Sometimes we subconsciously add to our memories of an event. Emotions may run high and can easily "fill in" details that were never there. For example, we may hear our parents' retelling of a fire that destroyed the family home. Their excitement can easily embellish the truth. The more often they retell the event, the more factual the embellishments become, both to them and also to the children who witnessed the tragedy through immature eyes.

Of equal importance in determining the validity of an event is the human tendency to omit parts of a happening. Memories can easily fade with the passing of time. If we were happy when the incident occurred, the subconscious mind typically searched for the positive characteristics and allowed any unhappy aspects to fade away. Conversely, if we were unhappy at that time, we tended to remember the negative traits and enlarged upon them. After the distorted memories (either positive or negative) were rehearsed a number of times, they became real to us. Sometimes the pain of remembering becomes so great that the subconscious mind simply denies the truth but the event, with all its emotions, is still circulating in the deep currents of the mind.

Elijah

An excellent example of distorted memories can be found in the biblical account of Elijah. Jehovah's fearless spokesman stood boldly before wicked King Ahab and predicted a drought over the entire land. After three years with no rainfall, Elijah boldly answered the king's inquiry, "Is that you, O troubler of Israel?" (1 Kings 18:17). Elijah challenged Ahab to send his 850 false prophets to meet him in a contest on Mount Carmel.

Every Bible student is familiar with the success of that encounter and Elijah's mad dash before Ahab's chariot to the entrance of Jezreel, where he stopped dead in his tracks at the words of wicked Queen Jezebel's messenger: "So let the gods do to me, and more also, if I do not make your life as the life of one of them by tomorrow about this time" (1Kings 19:2).

Jezebel was wicked; she meant what she said. Elijah ran for his life.

Jezebel was wicked and she meant what she said! Elijah ran for his life all the way from the northern part of the kingdom to the southern section. He finally stopped in the wilderness of Beersheba, where an angel provided food and water for his further journey to Mount Horeb.

It was at Horeb that the Lord questioned His servant. Elijah replied, "I alone am left; and they seek to take my life" (1 Kings 19:14). After some further instructions, the Lord reminded His servant: *There are yet seven thousand that have not bowed to Baal!*

Elijah's views were distorted, to say the least. He certainly did not have all the facts before making his marathon run in trying to escape Jezebel.

Summary

The brain is probably the most remarkable part of the human body. Within it are stored millions of memories that shape our lives.

The three primary kinds of memory are (1) *episodic memory*—an experienced event, (2) *somatic data*—bits of information, and (3) *procedural memory*—a recollection of how to perform a process.

The three stages of memory are (1) *holding*—the reception of raw data through the senses, (2) *short-term memory*—the brief storage of impulses received from the initial holding stage, and (3) *long-term memory*—the final storage place for selected memories from short-term memory.

The three processes in the saving of memories are (1) *encoding*—translation of sensory impulses to short-term memory over the connections between the nerves, (2) *storage*—the brain's selection of which impulses it wishes to save, and (3) the *retrieval* (recalling) of stored information.

Although memories reflect who we are, they may become *distorted* by our subconscious addition to or subtraction from the facts or even denial of those too painful to recall.

With a cursory knowledge of these basic facts about memory, we are now ready for the next chapter, which centers around unhappy memories and how to deal with them.

References

Frank Minirth, M.D., *The Power of Memories: How to Use Them to Improve Your Health and Well-being* (Atlanta, GA: Thomas Nelson Publishers, 2000).

Alma E. Guinness, Editor, *The ABC's of the Human Mind: A Family Answer Book* (Pleasantville, NY: The Reader's Digest Association, Inc., 1990).

Guy R. Lefrancois, *Psychological Theories and Human Learning: Kongor's Report* [Monterey, CA, Brooks/Cole Publishing Company (A Division of Wadsworth Pub. Co., Inc., Belmont, CA), 1972].

Questions for Thought

1. Discuss what God made on each day of creation.

2. In what significant ways do human beings differ from previously formed creatures?

3. Discuss the amazing power of the brain, especially as it adapts to new situations.

4. Factual happenings are stored in our memories along with their accompanying feelings and emotions. How can this fact color our memories?

5. Discuss the three primary kinds of memory and give an illustration of each.

6. What are the three stages of memory?

7. What is the holding capacity of short-term memory called? How many unrelated numbers normally form the limit that the short-term memory can hold at a time?

8. What are the three processes in the saving of memories? Illustrate each one.

9. Discuss how the following filters influence which memories are saved in storage: emotions, interest, distortion, denial, and erosion.

10. How do the factors of recognition, recall, and triggers influence the retrieval of memories?

11. How have our childhood memories helped shape the person we are today?

12. Does a child have the maturity to discern truth from error? How does this basic fact influence his childhood memories?

13. In what ways are our early memories prophetic?

14. In what three ways can memories become distorted?

15. Relate the story of Elijah's confrontation with the prophets of Baal on Mount Carmel.

16. Why do you suppose Elijah was so fearful of a woman?

17. How was Elijah's evaluation of the situation distorted?

18. Why is a basic understanding of the manner in which memory works essential to this study?

Jane, most intellectual,
high school

Most Intellectual
JANE SHANNON
and
BOBBY ELLIOTT

Mr. and Mrs. Don McWhorter,
1956

Litton High debate team:
Coach Prater, Jane, Joy Wiegant,
Roy Nash, Joe Holland

Don's team, 2nd place,
National Debate Tournament,
West Point, 1955

Building Bridges across Painful Memories

The previous chapter focused on some fundamental facts about memory. This chapter expands upon that foundation as it explores the causes of our painful memories, the healing of the unhappy ones, and dealing with those that will not heal.

How satisfying it is to reminisce about pleasant memories! Their recollection is as refreshing as a warm breeze on a spring day and brings much comfort. Most of the remaining chapters of this book will deal with developing an awareness of those comforting memories and learning how to cultivate and preserve them. However, if we are completely honest with ourselves, we must admit that there are *some* past events that bring us much pain. How do we deal with them? Dwell upon them until they consume our lives? Pretend they don't exist? Suppress them? Seek council from friends? Pay for professional help? Try to work our way through them?

Although it is true that we can't change the past, we need not be imprisoned by it. Even painful memories can be used as stepping stones in developing a stronger Christian character if only we deal with them wisely.

The Power of Long-Term Memories

Earlier in this study we briefly considered the dynamics of long-term memory and discovered that it is much like an underground river, continually flowing and shaping our characters.

Our basic personalities are usually molded by the time we are four years old. Those early memories shape the way we think as an adult and also the image we have of ourselves. Looking back on early years helps us understand our social preferences, our temperaments, our strengths, and our weaknesses.

The attics and basements of our minds can yield nuggets of gold or the poisons of painful memories.

The attics and basements of our minds can yield nuggets of gold or the poisons of painful memories. We take all past events with us throughout life—good and bad. They can be blessings or curses as we experience each new event, as we form our perceptions of life, as we set goals, and as we choose our mates. Sometimes memories are subtly hidden in the corners of our minds or they may be as evident as signs on the interstate.

Psychosomatic Illnesses

Poor health can be triggered by many different factors, but hidden painful memories may manifest themselves in our lives by attacking our physical bodies through psychosomatic illnesses. Most of us are familiar with the physical manifestations of stress, but these same symptoms can be generated by hurtful memories, which often produce anger or even guilt. The more common ones are headaches, intestinal problems such as ulcers and colitis, muscle aches and tensions, bad dreams and nightmares, anxiety, nervousness, irritability, unfounded fears, undue guilt, and inability to function normally. The list goes on and on, making the consequences of painful memories apparent.

Our emotions can cause the release of chemicals to aid in the recollection of past events. For decades we may not even think about a happening from long ago, only to discover that one small trigger—a snapshot, music, an aroma, a taste, or a faded letter—can cause that memory to surface at a most unexpected moment. As I mentioned at the beginning of this study, a flood of pleasant memories cascaded when my daddy found a crudely typed booklet summarizing the major stories of the Old Testament that I had put together during my elementary school days. Once again I could feel myself sitting at our kitchen table, and I almost heard the sounds of that old manual typewriter as I pecked with one finger.

Examples of Painful Memories

Every honest person has to admit having some painful memories, varying in intensity from one individual to another.

Perhaps those hurts were only slight—embarrassment over saying the wrong thing, humiliation by the thoughtless remarks of a teacher during the early years of life, the feeling of rejection by our peers at school because our clothes were different or we were not fully accepted by the "in" group.

Some painful memories can be quite severe—physical abuse as a child, an alcoholic parent, the devastation caused when parents divorced, rejection by a sweetheart during our young and tender years, emotional and physical pain in our own marriage relationship, a home destroyed by fire, financial loss, flashbacks of a horrible automobile accident, our adult children who no longer have anything to do with us, criminal harm to our families, the lingering death of a loved one, and splits in the Lord's church caused by people who no longer respect the authority of the word of God. On and on the list could go. These hurts, humiliations, and horrors can plague us for our entire lives unless, with God's help, we take control of our patterns of thought and put these memories in proper perspective.

The origin of other painful memories may be the result of our own faults. For example, we may suffer pangs of guilt over our own treatment of other people. At the time, we were oblivious to the hurt we were causing them. However, the passing of years can be a painful reminder of our thoughtlessness.

The Admission of Hurts

Some events are too painful to be dealt with at that moment. Because the hurts are so sharp, our emotional systems simply cannot handle them while they are fresh, so we try to push them to the back of our minds. The storing of painful memories may be necessary for a short time as we try to regain a normal life, but efforts to blot them out permanently can be devastating because their underground current is always flowing in our long-term memories. We must choose not to be victims. Sooner or later, perhaps when we are more mature and wiser, those events must be looked in the eye, acknowledged, and integrated with the rest of our lives before we can be happy and productive.

The mother of a victim of a violent crime thought she had dealt well with the hurt inflicted upon her child. In the beginning she had talked freely about the incident and had even counseled with parents facing similar tragedies. Years later, when she was called for jury duty and discovered that the case involved a similar crime, uncontrollable feelings came upon her as she gazed at the accused. Her heart started beating rapidly, her breathing became labored, and the tears started flowing. The hurt was just as fresh as the day she stood by her child's side in a police station many years earlier. Being called to jury duty evoked a fresh realization of the previous painful events as well as all the emotions that accompanied the original hurt. The underground river of memory flows continuously and can surface with only a slight trigger. This realization makes it important to get memories—even hurtful ones—in their proper perspective.

Treasures are constantly being washed up on the shore after the storms of life. Instead of complaining because they are irritating, we should open our eyes, realize their purpose, pick them up, and hold them close to our hearts.

The Inaccuracies of Memories

Before considering how to deal with hurtful memories, it is wise to realize that all those memories are not accurate. The conditions of life can affect the way we see an event. Drugs, alcohol, an aging mind, disease, trauma, and depression can alter our perception of a happening.

It must be remembered that a child lacks maturity, and he witnesses an event through a child's eyes. His perception of an adult can alter his memory. For example, his memories of a grandmother may have placed a halo around her head because that important person in his life was good to him; consequently, his perception of her blotted out most hurtful memories connected with the grandparent. An abusive parent, on the other hand, will always be remembered as hurtful, even though that parent undoubtedly did many good things for the child. His immature mind remembers only the hurt.

The hurt was just as fresh as the day she stood by her child's side many years earlier.

Most beliefs, whether true or false, are formed during childhood. Ken Wilson, Ph.D., is the author of an enlightening article printed in *Gospel Advocate* ("The Power of the Mind,"

September, 2005, p. 35). In that writing he quoted Dr. William Backus, author of *Telling Yourself the Truth:*

> It is not, however, events either past or present which make us feel the way we feel, but our interpretation of those events. Our feelings are not caused by the circumstances of our long-lost childhood or the circumstances of the present. Our feelings are caused by what we tell ourselves about our circumstances.

We must realize that memory is not always accurate. Several different witnesses at the scene of a crime may give different accounts of the events that transpired and, in their own minds, believe they are truthful. They all saw the same incident but focused on different details, remembering some and forgetting others. Family reunions are an example of this truth. In talking about events of years gone by, some saw one thing and others remember a different scene at the same incident. Sometimes two events inaccurately merge into one. We may have heard our parents' versions of happenings so many times that their distorted remembrances merge with our childish memories until they become factual to us.

Inaccurate Pictures Make Emotional Cripples

We have a tendency to remember what is meaningful to us. For example, on the day our new neighbors moved into the house across the street, I saw a group of five or six people in their driveway and stepped over to say hello to the new occupants of the house. A woman identified herself when I told the group that I had come to meet my new neighbors. I then focused on her name, her face, and personality characteristics because she was the person who was important to me at that moment. If my life depended upon it, now I would not be able to recognize any of the others standing in the driveway that day. They were there and I saw them, but I was not focusing on them. The same thing is true of many of our memories. We do not accurately remember the whole event.

Memories do not come neatly packaged as good or bad but are intertwined. We are constantly taking pictures of life and storing them in the albums of our memories. Because of our ineptitude, we may have used the wrong speed of film, light, or angle. The lens may have been dirty or we may have missed part of the scene. Perhaps we have overexposed the pictures or cut off part of the subject matter. Some are faded and blurred. Others may be in black and white while some are in colors.

It may be easy for us to go through the albums of our lives and think that these pictures are actual portrayals of events in our lives, but they may not always be ac-curate because we are just human and not professional photographers of life. We should not allow our amateur photography to make us emotional cripples all our lives.

> *We have no control over our genetic code or environment; we do have a choice over our memories.*

Our Choice

As mature people, we need to get those pictures from the top shelves of the closets of our minds and take a realistic look at them. We have no control over our genetic code or the envi-ronment into which we were born, but we do have a choice over how we perceive our memories. It depends upon our outlook on life and a realization of the gold that can be found in hurtful memories.

The story is told of a young rabbi who sought recognition from his villagers. Evidently his own opinion of himself was in-flated, but he couldn't seem to convince those around him of his wisdom and lofty position. In time he grew bitter.

One day an older rabbi, who was wise and respected, visited the village. The young rabbi schemed to get revenge by devising a test. He planned to put a small bird in the palm of his own hand and ask the older rabbi if the bird were dead or alive. If the older man said "alive," he would crush the bird to death before displaying it for all to see. If the older rabbi said "dead," then the young man would open his hand and allow the bird to fly away. He thought this test would earn him great respect.

The next day the younger man challenged the older rabbi by saying, "We know how wise you are, but can you answer my question? Is the bird in my hand dead or alive?"

The older rabbi was silent for a moment. Then with kindness he looked into the eyes of the younger man and observed: "It is up to you, my friend. It is up to you."

Just as the younger rabbi had the power over the fate of that bird, so do we have the power to make good come from our hurtful memories. Sometimes we have to travel through dark shadows to reach the point of victory. What we find at the end of that journey is up to us.

Sometimes we have to travel through dark shadows to reach the point of victory.

We have all heard stories of the horrors of Auschwitz during World War II. One of the prisoners, Victor Frankl, later observed that everything could be taken away from those prisoners of war but one thing—the freedom to *choose* their attitude in any given set of circumstances. Those who chose to rise above the horrors of the concentration camp survived. Those who could not muster that kind of strength did not make it. The same is true of all of us. We may not be able to control *what* happens to us, but we have the power to control *how we respond*. As the wise rabbi observed, "It is up to you." We have the power to crush our lives or set them free.

Rising above Adversity

Joseph

Joseph is a prime example of rising above painful memories. Few of us have ever experienced the rejection this young man received from his peers. The dark dampness of that pit into which he was thrown must have remained with him throughout his life. The look in the eyes of his brothers as the coins were being counted out when he was sold into slavery had to be indelibly etched in his mind, as were his feelings of helplessness as his masters led him away from his home into a foreign land.

Joseph's plight seemed to be improving when he was bought by an Egyptian named Potiphar and given charge of his master's household. The young slave's stroke of good fortune came to a dramatic end, however, when he stood up for his moral convictions and refused to commit adultery with his master's wife.

The walls of a prosperous household gave way to the horrors of prison, but Joseph's outstanding character was instrumental in securing for him a favored place of responsibility as the keeper of the prison. It was here that he interpreted the dreams of the chief baker and butler. The baker was to be put to death, but the butler was to be restored to his former position. Joseph had asked the butler to mention his name to Pharaoh when he was released. The butler forgot. Two full years passed while Joseph waited in vain for release. Imagine what kind of memories of those days he must have carried with him throughout life.

Every Bible student is familiar with Joseph's rise to the position of being second only to Pharaoh after he was finally released from prison, and we know all too well the story of the famine and his brothers' trip to Egypt to get food. But step across the threshold of Joseph's dwelling and vicariously witness the emotionally charged scene that transpired at the noonday meal when he saw his brothers, including Benjamin, his beloved younger brother. Joseph's relatives had not seen him since he was a teenager and did not recognize him. But Joseph certainly recognized them. Overcome with emotions, Joseph excused himself and wept outside the chamber. After releasing his feelings, the young ruler washed his face and composed himself before returning to the dining area. As he looked into his brothers' faces, we can only imagine the thoughts that must have gone through his mind. Sometimes we feel sorry for ourselves and think we have more trouble than anyone else, but think about all the hurtful memories Joseph must have had—rejection by his brothers, a dark pit, being sold into slavery, false accusations by Potiphar's wife, and the horrors of Pharaoh's prison, as well as being forgotten by the butler whom he had helped. How the sight of his brothers must have triggered all these painful memories!

It Was Not You, It Was God

Later, when Joseph made himself known to his brothers while openly weeping, he showed his godly character when he observed, "And God sent me before you to preserve a posterity for you in the earth, and to save your lives by a great deliverance. So now it was not you who sent me here, but God" (Genesis 45:7–8).

Years later, when Jacob died and the brothers asked for Joseph's forgiveness, he further pointed out the gold in the hurtful events of his life: "But as for you, you meant evil against me; but God meant it for good, in order to bring it about as it is this day, to save many people alive" (Genesis 50:20).

"God meant it for good!" How powerful! Because of Joseph's trust in God, he saw the world through a different pair of glasses. He was able to put painful memories behind him and get life in its proper perspective. Today God still gives Christians special lenses in their glasses. Because of His teachings, we are able to see hurts in a mature manner and rise above them.

Peter

Peter used his painful memory as a stepping stone. An earlier chapter in this study centers around the memories associated with the Lord's supper. On that dark night the impulsive fisherman caved in to pressure and repeatedly denied his Master.

As Jesus was being led from one area of the palace where His trial took place to another part of the building, Peter's adamant denial must have been audible: "Man, I do not know what you are saying!" (Luke 22:60). The cock's immediate crowing undoubtedly triggered Peter's memory of Christ's earlier foretelling of his desertion. Jesus "turned and looked at Peter" (Luke 22:61). Oh, that look! Undoubtedly the gaze of the Master triggered Peter's memory of the previous scene in which Christ foretold His apostle's denial. *Peter remembered.* He went out and wept bitterly.

Victor or Victim?

The Scriptures indicate that Judas must have also had bitter memories that same night after he had betrayed Christ for thirty pieces of silver. Matthew's account states that in the early hours of the next morning, when Judas realized that his Master had been condemned and was being led away, with a penitent heart he tried to return the blood money to the chief priests and elders. When they refused to take it and Judas realized the impact of his betrayal, he went out and hanged himself (Matthew 27:1–10).

> *Undoubtedly the gaze of the Master triggered Peter's memory. He wept bitterly.*

Judas had painful memories. He found an easy way out when he took his life. Peter also had painful memories, but his reaction to those memories led him down a different path.

Fifty days later, on the day of Pentecost, Peter was able to rise above his painful memories of that betrayal night when Jesus looked past this fumbling, weak apostle and saw the potential for the man he could become. Just as many present-day church buildings in Jerusalem are built upon the ruins of other buildings, so was Peter able to build upon the ruins and devastations of his own life to become a tower of strength for the early church.

Undoubtedly Peter's earlier memories were instrumental in the kind of man he became. As the wise rabbi stated in an earlier story, "It is up to you, my friend. It is up to you."

Questions for Thought

1. Discuss the following statement made near the beginning of this chapter: "Although it is true that we can't change the past, we need not be imprisoned by it." Do you agree or disagree?

2. What are some physical manifestations of hurtful memories?

3. Discuss some examples of painful memories that are part of life.

4. Give some examples of painful memories we can bring upon ourselves.

5. Sometimes we push painful memories into the back of our minds because they are simply too painful to deal with at that time. Is this method of coping good or bad?

6. Why are memories not always accurate? Cite some examples.

7. Relate the story of the young and old rabbis. What is the lesson for us today?

8. Imagine yourself as Joseph on his journey of life. Has anyone in the class faced as many hardships as this son of Jacob?

9. How could God have meant all of Joseph's trials "for good"? (Genesis 50:20).

10. Relate a personal instance of good coming from a bad experience.

11. Follow Peter through his denials by comparing the four Gospel accounts. How do you think you would have reacted if you had been walking in Peter's sandals that night?

12. Judas also must have had painful memories. Contrast the manner in which Judas and Peter handled their painful experiences. Do you think Peter's painful memories helped make him stronger? Why?

Debate honors for Don at
David Lipscomb College

MORRISON and DON McWHORTER are pictured with COACH CARROLL ELLIS at
West Point where they competed with thirty-three outstanding teams of the nation.

The McWhorter hearth,
Christmas, 1966

Don and grandson Jack, son of
Greg and Shannon, 2006

The McWhorter family:
Don, Jane, Kathy, Greg

It's Up to You!

If we are completely honest, most of us will have to admit that there are some deeply lurking and rather painful memories that surface from time to time from the underground streams of our minds. They won't go away because they are now, and forever will be, a part of us. They can either be crippling if we dwell on their negative aspects or be silver linings in those dark clouds, proving to be some of the greatest blessings of our lives. Memories need to be brought into our consciousness, accepted, and integrated into our lives so healing can begin. As the wise rabbi concluded in the previous chapter, "It's up to you, my friend. It's up to you."

Sometimes when painful events occur, stuffing them in the back of our minds seems to be the easiest solution at the time. The only problem is that they will eventually come out, sometimes when we least expect them. The memories that we carry in our hearts must, sooner or later, be met and resolved if we are to have peace with ourselves.

When our painful memories are caused by a wrong *we* have committed against another person or privately against God, nothing will even begin to ease the pain until we do what is right in God's sight. Confessing our mistakes to the person we have wronged, as well as to God, is necessary if we are to ever begin the path to peace (Matthew 5:23; James 5:16).

It may be necessary for these memories to be "reframed." They may not be accurate.

Often, however, we bear painful memories through no fault of our own. Sometimes they were fueled by the thoughtlessness or the cruelty of others. At other times they resulted from circumstances beyond our control—the vicissitudes of life.

It may be necessary for these memories to be "reframed." When the pictures were first snapped and imbedded in our hearts, they may not have been accurate. Our childish eyes may not have seen the whole scenario. Consequently, we forever carry the blemished imprint in our hearts, causing us much pain. Going back and looking at the events through mature eyes can sometimes reveal an entirely different story and help free us from hurt.

My Own Search

Those who have followed my writings throughout the years are aware that, through no fault of our own, our family was involved in a head-on collision a number of years ago. The wreck was caused by an inexperienced driver without a license who lost control of her car in the oncoming lane of traffic. Although the other members of our family were hospitalized for a week, my face was shattered into over two hundred fractures, later requiring bone grafting from two of my ribs into my eye sockets.

In addition to head injuries, I also suffered a broken back, hip, arm, and leg. My ten-month recovery time gave me ample opportunities to think as I tried to piece together the puzzle parts of what had happened to us.

Previous to that accident, my life had been relatively trouble free. As a young preacher's wife, I had often given advice to fellow Christians as they struggled to cope with their problems and accompanying painful memories. However, when it became my turn to try to find solutions to the eternally asked question of *WHY*, I discovered that the solutions are not always so readily apparent when the question is your own.

There were many times when I awakened in the stillness of the night, struggled with plausible solutions to the problem, and then either cried myself back to sleep or sat at our kitchen table for several hours as I put my thoughts on paper.

Peephole in the Fence

However, I slowly found my answers. How well I remember attending a Bible teachers' workshop in Chattanooga a few months after that wreck. I will never forget the words of the teacher.

> We are looking at the parade of life only through a small peephole in the fence. The picture we see may be distorted because it is only a tiny segment of the entire parade. Remember that God is also watching. From His vantage point, He sees everything from the beginning of time until the end of the world, whereas we just see a very small particle of life. The only thing that really matters is where we will spend eternity.

In other words, we need to get life in its proper perspective. Sometimes our painful memories seem large because we don't have the whole picture. We are wise if we reinterpret them in terms of the overall plot of life. That truth shaped my search.

Much as a mother shelters her unborn child within the warmth of her own body, I carried the seed in my heart of what later became *Let This Cup Pass* until it matured enough to exist apart from me.

As I speak to women throughout the country, many of them bring their well-worn copies of *Let This Cup Pass* for me to autograph. Time and again I have heard them say, "You have no idea how much this book helped me through a struggle in my life with so many bad memories that I have tried to overcome. This study seems to have been written just for *me*." It *was* written for each of us because, with a few variations, we *all* face the same basic core of problems in our lives at one time or another. We must never think that just because we have managed to get through one major obstacle in our lives, we will never have others. Problems are lurking around every corner. But the child of God has the responsibility to learn some basic coping techniques that will enable her both to handle the hurt and to grow from the experience.

None of us can escape problems. They are a part of life and their memories will always be in the underground streams of our hearts. Personally, I have found that getting painful memories in perspective is the best way to deal with them.

In this chapter I offer you the fruit of my heart.

Why, God?

Again and again people who are struggling with bitter memories cry out, "Why did God allow this hurt to come into my life? Isn't He powerful enough to spare me from all these painful memories?"

Yes, the God who parted the Red Sea for the escape of the Israelites from their Egyptian bondage has the power to spare His children from pain, but for a number of reasons He does not always choose to do so.

1. *To a certain degree God limited Himself in the garden when He gave Adam and Eve freedom of choice.* Their decision to eat of the

forbidden fruit resulted in expulsion from their earthly paradise. By choosing to eat the fruit of the tree of knowledge of good and evil, they consequently lost their opportunity to partake of the tree of life and live forever. At that moment death entered the garden, and Adam and Eve began the dying process. Barring an accident, most of us gradually die as various parts of our bodies wear out and we can no longer function.

2. *The laws of nature are consistent.* For example, fire can be quite beneficial in cooking food or providing warmth, but it can also be destructive. The laws of nature are consistent; fire will burn anything flammable in its path, even our houses.

Modern man is quite aware of the value of the use of steel in providing cars, airplanes, and buildings. But the hardness of steel is consistent. If it were not, buildings could collapse. When a steel beam falls upon a person, its hardness will probably result in injury or even death because the laws of nature are consistent.

Electricity offers untold benefits to mankind, but its laws are consistent. The power surging through those wires to heat our homes is no respecter of persons. When used without precaution, it kills people—both the good ones and the evil ones.

When hot and cold layers of air collide, storms and tornadoes result. Earthquakes deep within the ocean floor can produce tsunamis, killing thousands. Does God have the power to stop such catastrophes of nature? *Yes.* Did He ever promise that He would? *No.* The laws of nature are consistent.

Physical pain alerts us that something is wrong and we need help in alleviating the cause of the problem. That warning system is consistent.

> *Death entered the garden, and Adam and Eve began the dying process.*

3. *Our own carelessness is responsible for some of our problems with their accompanying painful memories.* Because we do not properly care for our bodies, we are faced with many illnesses. When we fail to heed the warnings of a traffic light, we may be struck by a car. On and on the list could go.

4. *Other people can cause deep emotional hurts.* Sometimes those hurts are provoked by our own carelessness in failing to nurture relationships, but often that is not the reason. In the beginning God decided that it was not good for man to be alone, so He created another human being for companionship. Today most of our pleasant memories center around our relationships with others. We would not want to endure life on this earth alone. Just remember, however, that other people are also free moral agents and have the freedom to choose their actions. They can be kind and supportive, but they can also be ruthless and hurtful. Most of the time they are just careless. All of us at one time or another have suffered because of the thoughtlessness and carelessness of others. Dealing with people, some of whom hurt us, is a part of life. When we tend to feel sorry for ourselves because of the way others treat us, we should reflect upon the way Jesus' closest friends turned against Him.

A baby needs to kick and exercise his leg muscles in order to walk; we need to exercise our spiritual muscles.

5. *Working our way through problems and painful memories can help us grow spiritually if they are handled properly.* Just as a baby needs to kick and exercise his leg muscles in order to be able to walk one day, so do we need to exercise our spiritual muscles if we are to develop into the kind of children God wants us to be. He loves us enough to do what is best for us. And it *is* best for us to learn how to cope with troubles because they *will* be there. They have been promised and are just a part of life.

God has told us that we *will* be tested (Job 14:1; John 16:33; 2 Timothy 3:12). During my days of teaching school, I usually told my students what material they should study to prepare for a test. On the day of the test, some of them looked at the questions on the exam as if they had never laid eyes on the subject matter. They had failed to prepare! God is going to allow the natural problems of life to test us: sickness, death of loved one, a house destroyed by fire, a wayward child, an automobile accident, financial loss, unjust criticism—on and on the list could go. Are we adequately preparing to meet those challenges?

Dietlinde Spears' Method of Coping

Many of you are acquainted with Dietlinde Spears through her books and lectures. Born in Silesia, Germany, her father was a member of the Nazi Party and held a high office in government. In January of 1945, the advancing Russian Army forced her family to flee on foot to Prague, Czechoslovakia. Few of us will ever face the hardships she endured during those days of the war and her subsequent days of living back in Silesia, East Germany, under Communism. Because of her victorious Christian spirit, I asked her to summarize how she managed to cope with such painful memories. She answered me in the following letter:

> I made a conscious choice to dwell on the few good things that happened to me during those horrible days of war, hunger and exposure to the elements. Someone shared a meal with someone, someone gave me a doll (a gift of love), someone took a risk of being seen and reported to the authorities and yet they came at night and brought a spoonful of sugar, or a little lard.
>
> I committed to my memory what was good and kind in people. I turned away from hate and vindictive behavior. Again, my commitment was a conscious effort.
>
> My little blessings helped my attitude to remain positive: an attitude I learned by refusing to become negative and pessimistic. I made myself look and think about beautiful and good hap-

penings and "things" (such as a pretty flower growing between demolished houses) even though I was among poverty, dirt, or in despair.

Naturally, after I became a Christian, prayer became my number one source. Everything became easier now; I did not have to consciously fight with my bad memories. I turned them over to God and received comfort and peace. The blessing of having a God who knows me, understands me, and who brought me out of misery to a great land like the USA is my greatest joy. Much can be forgotten with such a great God on my side.

> *"I did not have to fight with my bad memories. I turned them over to God and received comfort and peace."*

I truly believe my experiences, past and present, made me a stronger, more compassionate and understanding person. Prayer and trust in God is the answer to turn bad memories into joyous ones. Paul said, "In everything give thanks." Therefore, by thanking God for all of my experiences, I learned to see them as blessings for spiritual growth and commitment.

What a powerful letter! Our bad memories pale in comparison to those of this woman. If Dietlinde can do it, perhaps there is hope for the rest of us.

Put Painful Memories in Perspective

I will summarize the application of the material presented in this chapter by referring to the conclusion to *Let This Cup Pass*. After all my study and searching for the eternally asked question of *WHY*, I found my answer, which I condensed in the following allegory from a heart that has learned to trust. May it help you put your painful memories in perspective because, in reality, that is the only way to deal with them.

Once a child of the Master gleefully set about the task of weaving on a very large loom as her fumbling fingers learned to manipulate each thread handed to her by the Master Weaver.

"This is really no trouble at all," the youngster thought as she viewed the pleasant, sunny fabric she was weaving. Then the Master Weaver handed the child her first dark thread.

"What am I to do with this?" the novice asked. "I thought the Master's children were given only threads of the bright, sunny colors. This dark thread will ruin the cloth."

"You do not understand now, my child, but the dark thread is necessary. See what you can do with it."

Fumbling in anger and resentment over her assignment, the apprentice clumsily made an attempt to weave the dark color in and out among the bright hues. Her work was far from perfect, but the Master gave only encouragement. "That's fine, my child. You are learning. I merely ask that you try."

The next threads offered the young weaver were of her favorite bright color, and she heaved a sigh of relief that her dark thread was behind her. As she worked confidently with the brightly colored threads, the Master tapped her on the shoulder again and gave her another dark thread of a different hue. "But I have just finished using a dark one. Why am I given another one?"

"You may not understand, my little one, but I know best. See how well you can manage this one."

Having already dealt with one dark thread, the child knew all the frustrations involved with the task, but she loved her Master and believed He knew best, so the young one tried once more. Even she knew that her work was far from perfect but, because the Master seemed pleased with her efforts, she put her heart into the task.

As the days lengthened into years, the young child, who had now become a stooped, hoary-headed old woman, slowly came to expect the dark threads to be given to her from time to time along with the bright ones, and her resentment lessened. Weaving them into the tapestry became a challenge. She was so far removed from her first efforts that she could no longer even remember what they were like. She was too close to her present work to have any sort of perspective of the over-all picture.

After many years of tears, frustrations, and heartbreak, the broken old woman was called by the Master to cease her labors and rest with Him on a quiet, grassy hillside overlooking the valley where so many years had been spent at the loom.

"Faithful one, I have witnessed your heartbreak and frustration all this time with tears in My eyes, because I once was given a loom similar to yours upon which to weave. I also experienced sorrows and frustrations. But no one can enter my Father's house until he has mastered the art of daily weaving the threads on the loom of his life. I could see your mistakes, but I knew that you would learn if only you did not lose faith in Me and would keep on trying. I, too, had to learn to weave similar dark threads into my cloth. I remember how difficult they were to manage. Now that you can view your work from a distance, look at the loom upon which you have been weaving all these years."

As the broken form lifted her head to gaze upon the panoramic scene, she could scarcely believe her eyes. There were her first awkward attempts at using the dark threads. As her eyesight progressed from beginning to end, she was amazed at the beauty and perspective which the dark threads had given to her tapestry. She also noted how much more skillfully her pattern was woven as it neared the end.

"Now you can see what the dark threads have meant to your tapestry. Without them your cloth would have had no depth and beauty. Aren't you glad you had enough faith in Me to continue trying? Your years of weaving brought tears, frustrations, and disappointment. But you stayed with the task, never fully understanding the importance of those threads but trusting Me as I gave them to you. Now all your hard work is behind. My Father has prepared a wonderful place for you to live throughout eternity. Because you have remained faithful, there will be no more sorrow or pain. My Father will wipe away all tears from your eyes."

The Master gently gathered the frail, pain-ridden body of His child into His arms and entered a place more wonderful than any human being could possibly imagine. Never again would there be the arduous task of weaving—only eternal basking in the light of the Father's presence.

But the loom with the meaningful tapestry made of bright and dark threads was left in the valley with numerous others, including the perfect one of the Master Weaver. Many had been abandoned after a few unsuccessful tries, but some beautiful tapestries remained

as citadels of encouragement to other beginners that the task could be done if only they trusted the Master Weaver and faithfully kept on trying.

How have you handled the dark threads that are the lot of mankind? Have they given depth to your tapestry of life as you have allowed them to shape you into a more compassionate, mature Christian who has a better perspective and realizes that troubles are just a part of our lives? Have you grown spiritually and are you now able to give encouragement to others who are struggling with painful events in their lives? Or have you caved in to life's troubles and become a bitter, resentful person?

Remember the words of the wise rabbi: "It's up to you, my friend. It's up to you."

I Wish You Enough

Several years ago I read an article in *House to House*, edited by Allen Webster of Jacksonville, Alabama. It touched my heart, probably because it summarized what I had previously learned about getting unpleasant memories in perspective. The story goes something like this:

> Recently while I was waiting for a flight, I overheard a father and daughter in their last moments together. Her flight's departure had been announced. Standing near the security gate, they hugged.
>
> The elderly man said, "I love you. I wish you enough."
>
> She, in turn, said, "Daddy, our life together has been more than enough. Your love is all I ever needed. I wish you enough."
>
> They kissed, and she left. He walked over toward the window where I was seated. Standing there I could see he wanted to cry. I tried not to intrude on his privacy, but he welcomed me in by asking, "Did you ever say goodbye to someone knowing it would be forever?"

"Yes, I have," I replied. Saying that brought back memories of expressing my love and appreciation for all my Dad had done for me. Recognizing that his days were limited, I took the time to tell him face to face how much he meant to me. So I knew what this man was experiencing.

"Forgive me for asking, but why is this a forever goodbye?" I asked. The elderly man replied, "I am old, and she lives far away. I have challenges ahead. And the reality is that her next trip back will be for my funeral."

"When you were saying goodbye, I heard you say, 'I wish you enough.' May I ask what that means?" He began to smile. "That's a wish that has been handed down from other generations. My parents used to say it to everyone." He paused for a moment and, looking up as if trying to remember it in detail, he smiled again. "When we said, 'I wish you enough,' we were wanting the other person to have a life filled with just enough good things to sustain him," he continued. Then, turning toward me, he shared the following as if he were reciting it from memory:

> I wish you enough sun to keep your attitude bright.
> I wish you enough rain to appreciate the sun more.
> I wish you enough happiness to keep your spirit alive.
> I wish you enough pain so the smallest joys in life appear much bigger.
> I wish you enough gain to satisfy your wanting.
> I wish you enough loss to appreciate all you possess.
> I wish you enough "Hellos" to get you through the final "Goodbyes."

To me, those words very simply, but eloquently, summarize the ability to deal with unpleasant memories by getting them in their proper perspective because life is a mixture of both good and bad experiences. Each one has its place. How we handle them is up to us. As we close this chapter, I will simply say to the reader, "*I wish you enough.*"

Questions for Thought

1. Why is stuffing unpleasant memories into the back of your mind usually not the best way to ease the pain? Can this method sometimes be used for short-term relief?

2. When our painful memories are caused by our own wrong doing, what should we do? (Matthew 5:23; James 5:16).

3. What does the term *reframe* mean? How can this method be helpful?

4. Relate the story about seeing life through a peephole in the fence. How can viewing the parade of life from beginning to end be helpful in getting a proper perspective?

5. Is God powerful enough to spare His children from painful experiences? Why doesn't He?

6. How did God limit Himself in the garden when Adam and Eve sinned? When they were expelled from their paradise home, what was no longer available to them? What were the consequences?

7. Show how the consistency of the laws of nature (using the examples of fire, the hardness of steel, electricity, adverse weather, earthquakes, and physical pain) can bring suffering upon mankind, contrasting both the benefits and the problems.

8. How can our own carelessness be instrumental in promoting unpleasant memories?

9. Why do you think the careless or vindictive words of other people can be so painful? Do they hurt more than the memories brought on by an impersonal agent, such as an act of nature? Why?

10. Summarize the note from Dietlinde Spears. Discuss the reasons for her unpleasant memories and the methods she used to deal with them.

11. Discuss Dietlinde Spears' statement: "I truly believe my experiences, past and present, made me a stronger, more compassionate and understanding person." Do you think you would have had such a positive attitude if you had walked in her shoes?

12. In the allegory concerning the tapestry of life, what did the bright and dark colors represent? Why was the manner of weaving the threads left up to the weaver? Why is the development of the tapestry of our own lives left up to us?

13. How can the inevitable rocks in the roadway of our lives make us better?

14. Relate the story at the conclusion of the chapter: "I Wish You Enough." Why do we need some of both the good and the bad in our lives?

15. The key to dealing successfully with unpleasant memories is getting them in perspective. Discuss the meaning of the word *perspective*.

Jane and granddaughter Shannon, daughter of Kathy and Tony, 1991

Jane and grandson Jack, son of Greg and Shannon, 2005

McWhorter home, Fayette, Alabama, before pines were cut

1962: Big sister Kathy greets newborn Greg as Mom looks on

Hurts
Caused By
Other People

In the preceding chapter we looked at the effects of painful memories and how to deal with their hurts by getting them in a proper perspective and seeing them as the common lot of mankind. After going to God's Word and thinking about the matter, most of us can accept sickness, deformities, death, acts of nature—tornados, earthquakes, floods—houses being destroyed by fire, financial loss, and even the wicked acts of war and personal crimes against us as part of the calamities that have plagued mankind for centuries. Because there is no personal vindictiveness, we learn to live with these problems and work them into the tapestry of our lives.

However, there is one area that is much more difficult to accept. When people we know and trust turn against us with criticism and cutting words, or even physical violence, we find it extremely difficult to turn the other cheek and go on our way. The

Scriptures refer to the tongue as a sharp razor (Psalm 52:2), as a sword and arrows (Psalm 64:3), as well as the poison of serpents and asps (Psalm 140:3). Proverbs 18:8 warns, "The words of a talebearer are like tasty trifles, and they go down into the inmost body." Because their piercing words are a direct attack upon our self-esteem, it is only natural for us to hurt. Both our adversary's actions and words leave deep scars on our hearts as the painful memories linger.

Their piercing words are a direct attack on our self-esteem; it is only natural for us to hurt.

Unless we draw into a shell and isolate ourselves from society, hurts inflicted by other people are almost inevitable. With David we can say, "Even my own familiar friend in whom I trusted, who ate my bread, has lifted up his heel against me" (Psalm 41:9).

Before we go any further into this study, it is may be best to pause and realize that sometimes we deserve and need the criticism we receive. "He who hates correction will die" (Proverbs 15:10). Before we pity ourselves, it is best to try to examine the remarks objectively, realizing that we all do wrong at one time or another. It is quite possible that we are guilty of a fault that we had never before realized. (We seldom see ourselves as others see us.) We should never be ashamed to say we are wrong when we are at fault.

However, there are times when the words spoken against us simply are not true. They hurt us down into the core of our beings. We may push them out of our conscious thinking, but they won't go away because they have now taken their place in the underground stream of our subconscious minds. How can we deal with the problem?

Understanding Criticism

1. *We should try to understand the background of the person who has hurt us.* He or she may be rude and completely out of place, but we can forgive much more easily if we only stop and think about the background of our assailant as we try to feel the rocks in her pathway of life.

When a person constantly criticizes and finds fault with others, most of the time the cause lies within. William Blake said, "As a man is, so he sees." Studies show that the typical faultfinder has a *defective image of himself.* The only way some people feel important is by pulling others down. Because they have an unhealthy image of themselves, faultfinding has become a habit, a way of life with them. Any innocent bystander can be the object of their aggression. When their attacks are vented toward us, we should not take their criticism personally.

2. *Some faultfinders are self-righteous and fail to see their own mistakes.* Naturally, those people have little compassion for the mistakes of others.

3. *Some people have never learned to keep their mouths shut.* They speak without thinking. Often they fail to learn the facts before they spread a rumor about someone. Because they chatter constantly and carelessly, the law of averages eventually catches up with them. We could happen to be the innocent bystander who receives the venom of their remarks. Again, we should not take the criticism personally.

Handling Criticism

1. *Be rational.* Being criticized does not make us failures. It has been said that no one kicks a dead dog. Accept the fact that busy, active people are the ones who are criticized the most, not the mousy ones who cringe in the corner, afraid they will

make a mistake. Not everyone is going to love and admire us. Remember, all the people did not love Christ.

2. *Act instead of reacting.* It is only human nature to protect ourselves (much as a conditioned reflex) when we think harm is coming our way. The Christian, however, should have the spiritual maturity to plan her response instead of merely reacting when threatened by the remarks of others. We should not allow them to influence our reaction. No one can *make* us act a certain way. We are free moral agents and can decide how we will respond.

3. *Bite your tongue.* Someone has said, "Many things are opened by mistake but none so frequently as one's mouth." How true! It is only natural to lash at someone who hurts you, but we should be mature enough to control our tongues. Painful memories can hurt enough when caused by someone else. They do not need to be intensified by our own harsh words. Ecclesiastes 3:7 states that there is a time to keep silence and a time to speak. Proverbs 29:11 adds to this idea by stating: "A fool vents all his feelings, but a wise man holds them back." "He who restrains his lips is wise" (Proverbs 10:19). (Have you ever spoken angrily and in haste, only later to regret what you said?) As long as our thoughts are in our minds, they are ours to deal with as we see fit. However, once spoken words leave our lips, they float out of our reach like feathers in the wind.

Handling Painful Memories

Locking painful memories into our subconscious minds can poison our entire bodies. We may figuratively turn off the lights, lock the door, and throw away the key, but the memory never leaves.

1. *We should eventually choose to remember painful experiences.* Laying them aside during the initial hurt may be the only course

of survival for a time. However, if we do not eventually look our hurts in the eye and deal with them, we will probably become their prisoners as they continually plague us in our self-made torture chambers.

In Deuteronomy 5:15 the Israelites were told to remember their slavery as well as God's discipline in the wilderness (Deuteronomy 8:15). On the surface, it would seem that the best course of action would have been to put all thoughts about the Egyptian whips behind them. Seemingly, forty years of wandering in the wilderness with nothing to eat but manna and quail—and often a lack of water—could only conjure feelings of resentment. However, God told them to remember for a purpose—the providence of God in delivering them from their painful experience and in bringing them into the land of promise. We, too, can learn to put hurts in perspective as we look for the nuggets of gold.

God told them to remember for a purpose—His providence in delivering them.

2. *Take an objective look at the painful memory through the filter of Christian maturity.* The facts of the memory can never be changed, but our feelings and perceptions at the time of the incident can be seen in a different light. Remember that your memories are recorded only from your own standpoint. Try to step into the shoes of the other person. At the time of the hurt, you may have been too young to understand the difficulties your assailant was facing. If you had walked in her shoes, you could possibly have acted in the same way. Understanding one another's feelings can pave the way for forgiveness.

At the time, we may have been completely oblivious to our own shortcomings. Looking at the memory objectively can sometimes enable us to see the other side of the coin and realize that we must bear some of the responsibility for what happened.

3. *Some painful pictures in the caverns of our memories need to be reframed with an attitude of forgiveness.* Consider a few Bible examples. David certainly had his faults, among them his adultery with Bathsheba and the murder of her husband in an effort to cover their sin. Yet the inspired writer of Acts (Acts 13:22) cropped off part of the shameful picture of David's life by reframing it with forgiveness as he used the description of David found in 1 Samuel 13:14: a man after God's own heart. From the beginning, David wanted to walk in the ways of the Lord, and he continually confessed his wrongs in penitence. God was always willing to forgive.

Abraham was far from perfect. First, he lied about Sarah's being his wife by passing her off as his sister when they journeyed to Egypt in search of food. Later, doubting God's promise for an heir, he succumbed to Sarah's suggestion of a sexual relation with Hagar to produce a son. But the writer of Romans reframed the story of Abraham's life as one of triumphs, not failures (Romans 4:18–22).

Confronting Offenders

Should we confront our critics or try to overlook the hurt they caused us? So often their words were spoken in haste or uttered because tearing someone else down is the only way that person can feel superior. They criticize nearly everyone. Whenever it is simply a case of our hurt feelings because of the thoughtlessness of others, we should be mature enough not to allow the matter to become a point of friction between us.

However, when that person's treatment of me is a wrong that could cause her to be eternally lost, then it is my responsibility to go to her in a loving, caring manner. Certain guidelines should be observed when confronting someone about a wrong.

"He that handleth a matter wisely shall find good" (Proverbs 16:20 KJV).

1. *Arrange a meeting with the offender promptly.* Sometimes it is wise to wait a little while for "cooling off" and reevaluating the problem. Our maturity may come to the forefront, enabling us to realize that it was only our feelings that were hurt. However, Ephesians 4:26 urges the discussion of a matter before it has time to fester. Procrastination may very well lead to the harmful, smoldering embers of bitterness.

2. *Never approach anyone in an arrogant manner.* Instead, we should go to that person with the right attitude and be willing to admit our own mistakes as we ask for her forgiveness if we have committed a wrong. Acknowledge the fact that you have been hurt. Others may not even be aware of the pain they have caused. If that person has committed a wrong that could cause her to be lost eternally, we should tell her about it in a nonthreatening manner as we speak the truth in love (Ephesians 4:15).

> *Refrain from saying, "You always . . ." or "You never . . ." Rarely are they true and they cause resentment.*

3. *Arrange a private setting for the initial meeting.* Thoughts will flow more easily between just the two of you.

4. *Choose your words wisely.* They are powerful. Compliment sincerely and freely. Use a lowered voice. "A soft answer turns away wrath, but a harsh word stirs up anger" (Proverbs 15:1). Refrain from making blanket statements such as "You always . . ." or "You never . . ." Rarely are such accusations true, and they tend to stir up resentment. Be open about your hurts as you talk with your critic.

5. *Listen patiently to the other person's point of view.* Perhaps you had never thought about the matter from her perspective.

6. *Join hands and pray.* There is healing in joining hands and taking our disagreements before the throne of God as we ask for His help in resolving our problems.

Sometimes a matter can be resolved immediately and the relationship can become even stronger because of the baring of our hearts to one another. On the other hand, time may be required to rebuild the trust we once had. Be patient.

Nathan Confronts David

David was not perfect. His sin with Bathsheba was inexcusable. In 2 Samuel 12, Nathan confronted David face to face. Note how the wise spokesman of God handled his encounter with the king. Instead of reproaching David behind his back, he went directly to the king. His words were based upon facts rather than rumors. Rather than criticizing David for his wrongs, he chose his words wisely, clothing his remarks in the form of a story about two men, one rich and one poor, and the slaying of the poor man's one little ewe lamb.

Evidently neither David nor Nathan held any hard feelings against one another after this confrontation.

Nathan's strategy went straight to David's heart, resulting in his pronouncing his own curse: "As the Lord lives, the man who has done this shall surely die!" (2 Samuel 12:5).

Nathan was well aware that David had the power to take his life. Boldly, he looked his king in the eye and proclaimed: "You are the man!" (2 Samuel 12:7). When David acknowledged his sin, Nathan told him of

God's forgiveness: "The Lord also has put away your sin; you shall not die" (2 Samuel 12:13).

Evidently neither David nor Nathan held any hard feelings against one another after this confrontation. When Solomon, the second child of David and Bathsheba, was born, Nathan gave him a special name: Jedidiah, which meant "beloved of the Lord" (2 Samuel 12:25).

When Relationships Won't Heal

Sometimes the situation does not end as well as the encounter between Nathan and David did. The relationship has been shattered and is never again the same. When we have sincerely tried to make wrongs right and the other person refuses, then we must commit to a course of action that will enable us to rid ourselves of the hurts and go on with our lives.

All too often we hold on to the pain, rehearsing it over and over in our minds until it eats at the very core of our lives. If we do not let go, we become the other person's slave. The memory of that wrong continues with us during every waking minute and everywhere we go. Bitterness becomes our master. But sooner or later, we must release its hold on us and get on with our lives. Let it go! (Ephesians 4:31).

Sometimes the hurt is so deep that we cannot handle it alone. What a comfort it is to acknowledge our inadequacy and rely upon God for strength to do what we know we must do.

Jesus' Suffering and Ours

We live in a world of imperfect people. Some are continually negative, disagreeable, irritable, and abrasive. It is not just a clash of personalities. These are difficult people who never seem to get along with anyone. They will probably go to their graves angry and irritable. We should never allow such people to pull us down as they try to draw us into their mode of thinking. As

Christians, we should certainly never resort to acting in the same manner as they do.

How many of us encounter the kind of treatment Jesus received? Not only did the mob turn against Him but also some of His own personal friends. Throughout these ordeals, He did not waver. Never did He allow the behavior of others to influence what He did or change His attitude of love into one of hate. Despite His knowledge that Judas would betray Him, He still washed the feet of that apostle. Peter, one of His closest friends, denied Him. In Luke 22:61 we are told that Christ turned to look upon Peter following his denial. (Have you ever wondered how much disappointment must have permeated that gaze?) On the cross Christ still exhibited an attitude of love as He interceded for the forgiveness of those who were crucifying Him. Never should we forget that evil is conquered by doing good (Romans 12:21).

Conclusion

As Christians we should do our best to resolve conflicts with other people in a manner that is pleasing to God. Frequently, going to that person with the right attitude in an open discussion of our differences and the confession of our hurt can clear the air. We should not allow their conduct to influence our own behavior. Instead, we should return good for evil.

Sublimation

If nothing else good comes from an unhappy encounter with someone, we can always find one nugget of gold: *We can become a better person by resolving never to treat another person as we have been treated.* When all efforts at resolution are futile, sublimation may be useful. Sublimation means "out of this world." In chemistry some solids can be sublimated; that is, they change into a gaseous state without becoming liquid. Such solids become sublime or of a higher order than their original state. Instead of harboring bitter, resentful memories, those who have been hurt can throw their energies into an effort that would lift them to a higher plain. For example, the child of an abusive parent can resolve that his own home will be Christ-like. The mother of a victim of a drunk driver can become a spokesperson for *Mothers Against Drunk Drivers*. The child of an alcoholic father can refuse to follow in her parent's footprints as she sets a proper example for her own children. The process may be long and arduous, much like traveling through a dark forest before coming into the sunlight of acceptance. Instead of being victims, we can be transformed into loving, wise, and mature people through our painful experiences.

Instead of being victims, we can be transformed through our painful experiences.

Rather than harboring harsh feelings against someone in our memories, we should try to remember those qualities that attracted us in the first place. If we are wise, we will search for these happy memories, place them close to our hearts, and then let the rest go out to sea as part of the ebb and flow of life. Remember that we are composed of bits and pieces of everyone who has ever crossed our paths. We alone are the ones who determine whether we choose to keep the good or the bad. It is our decision. A forgiving spirit does not erase painful memories. The emotional scars will always be there, but we can choose not to allow those memories to cripple us. Remember that memories are our teachers in the school of life. But we have to train ourselves to listen to their lessons.

Questions for Thought

1. Why do you think it is more difficult to deal with painful memories caused by other people than it is to accept the natural disasters of life?

2. To what is the tongue compared in Psalm 52:2; Psalm 140:3; and Proverbs 18:8?

3. Before we begin defending ourselves against criticism, why is it wise to look at the charge objectively? Why is this sometimes difficult?

4. Give three insights that may help us understand a person who is continually critical.

5. The lesson listed three suggestions for handling unjust criticism. Discuss them.

6. Sometimes a memory is so painful that we must put it aside for a time. Why is it to our advantage to eventually examine it?

7. Why did God tell His people to remember their days in Egypt and in the wilderness? (Deuteronomy 5:15; 8:15).

8. What is the advantage of looking at our painful memories through the filter of Christian maturity?

9. What is meant by the term *reframing*?

10. When is it wise to simply overlook hurtful words?

11. When a person's treatment of us is a wrong that could cause her to be lost eternally, what should we do?

12. Discuss the six guidelines for talking with someone who has wronged us.

13. What approach did Nathan use when he confronted David about his sin with Bathsheba? What was the result?

14. What should a Christian do when she has sincerely tried to make matters right between herself and one who has hurt her, and the dispute remains unresolved?

15. Discuss some of the painful memories that Christ must have endured.

16. What does the term *sublimation* mean? How can it help us live with hurtful memories?

17. How can painful memories be our teachers in the school of life? How can we train ourselves to listen to them?

*Wedding: Greg McWhorter and
Shannon Baldwin, 2003*

*Fall Creek Falls, Pikeville, TN:
Don and Jane's picnic area when
dating*

*Jane and granddaughter Emily,
daughter of Kathy and Tony*

Awareness of Everyday Blessings

The remainder of this book deals with one of the most effective tools for handling painful memories. Instead of allowing our hurts to cripple us, it is far better to use positive thoughts to fill the vacuum left behind by mended and banished memories. Jesus often used stories about everyday life to make a divine truth understood and remembered. I would like to use some thoughts found in a play written by Thornton Wilder to introduce this chapter of our study. During my college days I saw the play produced, and it left a lasting impression on my memory. I believe you will agree it teaches a powerful lesson.

Our Town

The setting for the story was Grover's Corners, a quiet little town of 2,642 people, nestled in the mountains of New Hampshire. The beginning time was the year 1901, during horse and buggy days. There was nothing particularly noteworthy about Grover's Corners—just the activities of ordinary people.

"Do any human beings realize life while they live it?— every, every minute?"

Act I vividly portrayed daily life in a town where nobody locked the doors at night. Most of the drama centered on the lives of two families who were next door neighbors. Dr. Gibbs and his wife Julia had two children: George and Rebecca. Charles Webb, the editor and publisher of the town newspaper, and his wife Myrtle also had two children: Emily and Wally.

Act II focused on the courtship and marriage of two of the children of these neighbors, George Gibbs and Emily Webb, and culminated with their wedding in 1904.

Act III began nine years later in 1913 with the funeral of Emily, who died in childbirth, leaving behind a four-year-old son and a grieving husband. Very uniquely the scene shifted to a conversation among the dead in the cemetery on a windy hilltop overlooking the sleepy little town as Emily made her way into the realm of those who had already passed away.

Just One More Day

As Emily talked with her departed acquaintances about what life was like among the dead, she expressed a desire to return to the earth for just one more day. They all discouraged her, telling her that she would be disappointed. But she insisted, choosing to relive the day of her twelfth birthday. The dead warned her that she would relive it with the full realization of the future.

Emily was delighted as she walked down Main Street as a spirit to the white fence that surrounded her home place. Entering the house of her childhood, she soon saw her mother coming down the stairs to start breakfast for her family. The spirit of Emily watched as the family ate their breakfast together and presented some birthday presents to the twelve-year-old while chattering about the upcoming events of the day. Because Emily's spirit knew what the future held as she observed the scene that morning, she was painfully aware at that time that her brother would die a short time later on a camping trip because of a ruptured appendix.

Time to Look at One Another

The words of Emily's spirit jar our complacency:

> I can't. I can't go on. It goes too fast. We don't have time to look at one another. I didn't realize. So all that was going on and we never noticed. Take me back—up to the hill—to my grave. But first: Wait! One more look. Goodbye, goodbye, world. Goodbye, Grover's Corners . . . Mama and Papa. Goodbye to clocks ticking . . . and Mama's sunflowers. And food and coffee. And new-ironed dresses and hot baths . . . and sleeping and waking up. Oh earth, you're too wonderful for anybody to realize you.

Through her tears Emily asked a question that should haunt each of us: "Do any human beings ever realize life while they live it?—every, every minute?"

Sadly, if we are honest, most of us would have to answer "No." We don't realize what blessings everyday life has to offer. In our frantic busyness we let many nuggets of gold slip through our fingers because we fail to capture, or even notice, the moments of our daily living.

Sounds of Life

When I recently reread *Our Town*, two words caught my eye—*clocks ticking*. During the eight-month period just before my mother died, our family exchanged audio cassette tapes with my parents after rheumatoid arthritis crippled my mother's hands and she could no longer write letters.

How thankful I am that we did not tape over *all* of them because they hold the key to some very precious memories. During those days each family would turn on a tape recorder and talk about everyday happenings: events going on at school, going to a carnival and buying a "bargain" guitar with only two strings, finding puppies in the woods behind our house, my daddy demonstrating to the children how he called squirrels in his side yard, my mother telling about the everyday events of their lives and even singing some of her favorite songs to her grandchildren, our son making our dog growl for his grandparents, water running in the kitchen sink as dishes were being washed, the dog howling when Don hit certain notes on the organ, our children fussing with one another. Life. Everyday life. No special occasions like birthdays or Christmas holidays. Just life. The days we take for granted.

The sounds of everyday life. The days we take for granted.

Minutes Ticking Away

During my parents' last two tapes, the nearby clock on the dresser in the bedroom of my mother and daddy was ticking very audibly. At the time, I didn't think much about it, but my mother passed away very suddenly soon after the last tape was made. When my sorrow would eventually allow me to listen to those tapes once again, I discovered that I was holding a priceless possession—the moments of everyday life over a seven-month period. Those minutes ticked away, but we were not even aware just how precious they were.

As Emily cried out in *Our Town*, "Do human beings ever realize life while they live it?—every, every minute?" Perhaps a few do. Those tapes helped make me more acutely aware of each moment of life. From time to time, as I am doing some routine cleaning tasks or riding in the car, I listen again to our family talk about their daily lives. Priceless!

Divine Awareness

The very first chapter of the Bible tells us that Jehovah was aware of the beauty of everything that was around Him. Beginning at the end of the third day of creation after the dry land appeared with its lush greenness, God saw "that it was good" (Genesis 1:12). After creating the sun, moon, and stars on the fourth day, the Almighty saw "that it was good" (Genesis 1:18). Evidence of the culmination of His awareness of beauty may be found at the conclusion of the sixth day in Genesis 1:31: "Then God saw everything that He had made, and indeed it was very good."

God's day-by-day awareness of the beauty of the world around Him should be a wake-up call for all of us to open our eyes and notice the preciousness of everyday life.

David's Awareness

David's solitary early years were spent on the hillsides near his home as he tended his family's flocks. No doubt day after day of witnessing the sun's first rays peeping over the horizon, as well as the last ones before the stillness of the night cast its evening shadows, imprinted their beauty on his heart.

These earlier scenes must have prompted David's words of appreciation for the beauty of nature in many of his psalms, such as those found in Psalm 19: "The heavens declare the glory of God; and the firmament shows His handiwork." Psalm 8:3 speaks of the beauty of the heavens, the moon and the stars.

In Psalm 143:5 David mused, "I remember the days of old." One cannot help but connect the *days of old* with 2 Samuel 23:2–4. Although David was speaking of the Messiah yet to come, his words are also applicable of any ruler of God, including himself.

> He who rules over men must be just, ruling in the fear of God. And he shall be like the light of the morning when the sun rises, a morning without clouds, like the tender grass springing out of the earth, by clear shining after rain (2 Samuel 23:3–4).

Close to the Shepherd

David was old. He was dying. The walls of his Jerusalem palace were cold and damp. He had experienced many joys but also numerous heartaches as even his own family turned against him. But somewhere back in the deep recesses of David's subconscious being, scenes from his early life on those lonely Judean hills when he tenderly cared for his sheep must have flashed across his mind: the freshness of the light of early morning at sunrise, a blue cloudless day, or drops of rain on tender spring grass. Perhaps David could forget those troublesome latter years as his thoughts transcended the ages.

Again he was close to his own Shepherd as he mentally returned to earlier carefree days and once more walked with His God. (Taken from my book, *Meet My Friend David*, 76.)

Did David realize the beauties of life while he lived it? Probably so.

Developing Our Own Awareness

I have had a number of wonderful instructors during my lifetime, but one truly stands out in my mind. My eighth grade teacher had a rather unique way of teaching poetry. No one in the class was ever required to memorize poetry. Instead, we were given a selected poem of literary merit at the beginning of each month to place in a special notebook and illustrate with a picture or an original drawing. Every morning the class read in unison the poem for that month. Each Friday we read not only the new poem but also the ones from previous months. To this day I can still recite almost all those nine poems. One of them has been especially meaningful to me.

Barter

Life has loveliness to sell,
All beautiful and splendid things.
Blue waves whitened on a cliff
Soaring fire that sways and sings.
And children's faces looking up,
Holding wonder like a cup.

Life has loveliness to sell,
Music like a curve of gold,
Scent of pine trees in the rain,
Eyes that love you, arms that hold,
And for your spirit's still delight,
Holy thoughts that star the night.

Spend all you have for loveliness,
Buy it and never count the cost.
For one white singing hour of peace
Count many a year of strife well lost.
And for a breath of ecstasy
Give all you have been or could be.

—Sara Teasdale

Life does indeed have loveliness to sell—the beauties of nature, a campfire that sways and sings, the wonder in the eyes of a child, relaxing music, the warm embraces of those dearest to us, communing with God through prayer and His Word. Or as the writer of *Our Town* pointed out—clocks ticking, Mama's sunflowers, the aroma of delicious food, freshly brewed coffee in the morning, newly ironed clothes, hot baths, sleeping and waking up. Memories don't have to be made out of spectacular events. Instead, the primary ingredients are just the ordinary, common, everyday blessings of life.

As Sara Teasdale expressed the thought,

> Spend all you have for loveliness.
> Buy it and never count the cost.

Ironically, the best things in life are not for sale. The only cost is the taking of our time to become aware of them. They are waiting for us to notice them and take them into our hearts. Sadly, most of us are too busy to realize all the blessings we have each day as we walk right by them without ever even noticing them in the pathway of our lives.

For a number of years I have kept the following meaningful words in my Bible. They have a message that has helped me become more aware of the blessings of everyday living.

The Station

Tucked away in our subconscious is an idyllic vision. We see ourselves on a long trip that spans the continent. We are traveling by train. Out the windows we drink in the passing scene of cars on nearby highways, of children waving at a crossing, of cattle grazing on a distant hillside, of smoke pouring from a power plant, of row upon row of corn and wheat, of flatlands and valleys, of mountains and rolling hillsides, of city skylines and village halls.

But uppermost in our minds is the final destination. On a certain day at a certain hour we will pull into the station. Once we get there so many wonderful dreams will come true and the pieces of our lives will fit together like a completed jigsaw puzzle. How restlessly we pace the aisles, condemning the minutes for loitering—waiting, waiting, waiting for the station.

"When we reach the station, that will be it!" we cry. "When I'm 18." "When I buy a new Mercedes Benz!" "When I put the last kid through college." "When I have paid off the mortgage!" "When I get a promotion." "When I reach the age of retirement, I shall live happily ever after."

Sooner or later we must realize there is no station, no one place to arrive at once and for all. The true joy of the life is the trip. That station is only a dream. It constantly outdistances us. "Relish the moment" is a good motto, especially when coupled with Psalm 118:24: "This is the day which the Lord hath made; we will rejoice and be glad in it." It isn't the burdens of today that drive men mad. It is the regrets over yesterday and the fear of tomorrow. So, stop pacing the aisles and counting the miles. Instead, climb more mountains, eat more ice cream, go barefoot more often, swim more rivers, watch more sunsets, laugh more, cry less. Life must be lived as we go along. The station will come soon enough.

—Robert Hastings

Conclusion

This particular chapter has not been intended to be scholarly or even a detailed search of the Scriptures. Before we devote time to a study of making cherished memories, I simply encouraged us to become more aware of each nugget of gold that is already there in our everyday lives. All of us will be blessed when we take a good look at these simple blessings and treasure them in our hearts. Each day is an opportunity to make a new start, putting painful memories in perspective as we remember the happiness of yesterday's blessings and look forward to the opportunities and challenges that are yet to be. Most important, we should fully relish the joy of this new day, being aware of all the bountiful blessings God sends our way.

I would like to conclude with a few more lines that have been written in the front of my Bible, because they have been meaningful to me for many years.

The days come and go, but they say nothing.
If we do not use the gifts they bring,
They carry them as silently away.

—Emerson

Questions for Thought

1. How can positive thoughts fill the vacuum left behind by mended and banished memories?

2. Briefly relate the plot of the play *Our Town*.

3. How would you answer Emily's question: "Do any human beings ever realize life while they live it?—every, every minute?"

4. This lesson discussed some audio tapes we exchanged with my mother and daddy during the seven-month period of time before her death. Today families make videos of birthdays, holidays, and other special occasions, but what about some sort of permanent recording of everyday life? What can you capture?

5. Read Genesis 1:12; 1:18; and 1:31. What was God's evaluation of His creation?

6. Describe what must have been the beauty of David's early life as he tended his sheep. Note Psalm 19:1 and Psalm 8:3.

7. Second Samuel 23 relates the last words of David. Although he was speaking of the Messiah yet to come, his words in verses 3–4 reflect the scenes of his childhood as he remembered the days of old (Psalm 143:5). Which of his descriptive phrases are most meaningful to you?

8. List the examples of loveliness found in Sara Teasdale's *Barter*.

9. "Spend all you have for loveliness. Buy it and never count the cost." What is the cost of loveliness?

10. Summarize the primary thrust of the selection *The Station*. Do you agree or disagree?

11. Read Emerson's words at the conclusion of this lesson. What gifts does each new day bring? What will happen if we are too busy to be aware of them?

12. How has this lesson made a difference in your life?

Ladies' day, Martin, TN, 2003: Janie Craun, Jane, Peggy Coulter

Kathy and daughters, Shannon and Emily, 1995

Wedding: Kathy McWhorter and Tony Kendall, 1987

Quilting Memories of Home

Some of the most important accomplishments of civilizations have been nurtured within the walls of its homes. For centuries the next generation has been trained to assume its responsibilities in the future years. Although the husband is the designated leader of the home (1 Corinthians 11:3; Ephesians 5:23), the charge to guide and keep the home running smoothly is ultimately the wife's responsibility (1 Timothy 5:14; Titus 2:4). She is generally the one who has the nurturing instinct and compassion to care for the members of her family.

The Virtuous Woman

Proverbs 31 outlines the qualities of an ideal woman. Her character was impeccable. The energy she expended in running her household was amazing. She had great wisdom and foresight in caring for her family as she planned, not only for their daily needs but also for their future necessities. Her sense of good business was evident as she bought property and sold the products of her home.

For the purpose of this chapter, let's consider her skills in dealing with cloth. "She seeks wool and flax, and willingly works with her hands" (Proverbs 31:13). Instead of buying woven cloth, she probably secured wool from her family's own flocks and flax from their own fields to make the cloth she needed. Not only was she efficient but she was also cheerful as she willingly went about the task of weaving cloth.

Verse 19 continues a description of the virtuous woman's skill in making cloth: "She stretches out her hands to the distaff, and her hand holds the spindle." The spindle and the distaff were the most ancient of all the instruments used for spinning thread. Adam Clarke sheds additional light on the skill of spinning when he comments:

> She takes the distaff, that on which the wool or flax was rolled; and the spindle, that by twisting of which she twisted the thread with the right hand, while she held the distaff in the guard of the left arm, and drew down the thread with the fingers of the left hand (Clarke's Commentary, Vol. III, p. 792).

It is apparent that the skill of spinning was acquired by much practice.

Because of her diligence, her family had no fear of winter's chill (v. 21). The virtuous woman's skill is further emphasized in verse 22, where we learn that she made coverings of tapestry and clothing of silk and purple. She made tapestry and carpeting, or quilted work for the beds and for her guests to sit upon. Also, her clothing was of the finest materials and colors.

Not only was the virtuous woman's family cared for, she also produced fine linens and girdles, wide belts worn around the middle of their loose robes, which she sold for profit (v. 24).

Coverings in a Previous Century

Today quilts are treasured works of art, but in previous generations they were also considered a necessity. There was no Wal-Mart to supply cover when the winter winds began to howl. No electric blankets were available to warm the beds. Instead, the mothers and grandmothers assumed the responsibility of making quilts to keep their loved ones comfortable in chilly houses. Before the glowing embers of a hearth, these women rocked and pieced together stacks of softly faded bits of material. Because buying new material would have been an extravagance, quilts were usually made from the family's outgrown or worn-out clothing, in addition to scraps of material from the making of a new dress or shirt. Each piece was a recollection of shared moments of laughter and tears—the dress Susie wore on her very first day of school, the shirt Tommy wore the day he was baptized, the blanket that kept a precious baby warm, great-grandmother's favorite apron.

Take time to view each new day as an opportunity to make new memories.

With stitches of unconditional love, mothers invested their time in joining together so many reminders of their families' lives—the ordinary moments they shared together, the minutiae of life. Fortunate are the children who grow up with the knowledge that their parents not only wanted them but also will love and cherish them throughout their lives.

Modern Quilt Makers

In a sense, we women can still be the quilt makers of our homes, if we will take the time to view each new day as an opportunity to make new memories as we treasure even the smallest moments. What a blessing it is to realize that what we are doing at this moment is exactly what we want to be doing. Delightful memories can be made from the ordinary events of life if only we become aware of their value—freshly baked cookies, a listening ear for the events of the day at school, heart-to-heart talking, watching a sunset, smelling flowers, catching lightning bugs with our children, a bedtime story, and good-night kiss with the scent of a mother's love. Unconditional love says, "I love you," "I'm sorry," and sometimes even "No."

One of the most valuable legacies we can leave our children is the gift of memories—memories of a home filled with love, God-given values, cherished traditions, and joyful celebrations. Children need good memories to stock their cellars for the long winter of life. The threads of love should bind together those who live under the same roof. Home should be a place of refuge from the world, a haven of belonging. Familiar sights and aromas are there to bring comfort in later years, even when the world is not always kind.

Home should be a place of refuge from the world, a haven of belonging.

Many springboards for making precious memories surround us but we seldom notice them. The opportunities for making treasures are waiting for us to take the time to become aware of their potentiality. Sadly, all too often we race through life at a break-neck speed and trample underfoot most of the chances to create special memories for our loved ones.

Quilt making is not cheap. Instead, it requires endless amounts of time and energy as the quilt maker commits herself to the task. She must remain faithful, even though progress may be slow at times.

Patterns Necessary

Some sort of pattern or plan is necessary for most work to be successful. Explicit directions were given for the construction of the tabernacle from the length, width, and height of all its parts to the kind of cloth to be used as coverings. In addition, patterns were given for the mercy seat, the altar, and even the clothing of the high priest (Exodus 25–28). The writer of Hebrews further emphasized the importance of the pattern shown to Moses on the mount when he explained the superiority of the second covenant (Hebrews 8:5).

Quilts also must have patterns. Although the pieces of cloth may have come from many different sources, there would be no beauty in a quilt if those pieces were sewn together without a pattern. As mothers, we have been given the responsibility of guiding the home and of deciding what will be the pattern of our patchwork quilt of memories. What are your plans for a pattern? If you have none, don't be too upset if you are disappointed in your family years from now. Fortunately, it is never too late to begin.

Making Memories with Our Husbands

When a man and woman marry, they just can't find enough minutes to spend with each other. They want to talk for hours on end, do special things together, and lavish gifts upon one another to express their love. As time passes by, the man and, quite frequently, his wife become caught up in the demands of their jobs. Tired at the end of a long workday, they no longer look for opportunities to be with one another. Indifference sets in.

Then the children arrive! There are wakeful babies to be walked at night, toddlers to oversee 24/7, spelling words to call out in preparation for a test, children to be transported to ball games and after-school events, and teenagers to be guided, even when they don't want to be guided. When the last child leaves home, a husband and wife may find themselves living with a virtual stranger because they have neglected the hub of the home: their relationship with one another. When the only common interest a husband and wife share is their children, their marriage is in danger.

Love Their Daddy

I have often told women that the most important gift they can give their children is the love that their mother and daddy share for each other. If that relationship is secure and is placed even above their love for the children, then all other problems in the home fall into place and become manageable.

Times have changed. Days used to be filled with hard physical work. However, when the supper dishes were washed and put away, families had time to relax and talk before bedtime, as they listened to the rhythmic creak of the rope on the swing on the front porch instead of dashing off to various commitments. Husbands and wives still need periods of time when nothing special is planned—times when they can walk along together, hand in hand, and enjoy the beauty of a sunset.

Couples vary in their interests. What sounds exciting to one may be boring to another. Some husbands and wives enjoy going to sporting events together. Others may find no pleasure in rooting for their favorite team. Some couples enjoy a quiet evening together at an elegant restaurant. Others prefer dinner at McDonalds. The important thing to remember is that we all need to spend some quality time with each other as we engage in an activity that is mutually enjoyable. The busier we become with our children, the more important it becomes to schedule some "date" time with our mates—dinner, a sporting event, travel, or a weekend getaway.

Prevent Marriage Chills

Children make a lot of demands, not only on our time but also on our billfolds. There are always school shoes to buy, orthodontist's bills to be paid, and college expenses looming ahead. It is just as important to regularly set aside some money for a husband and wife to be with one another as it is to pay the electric bill. If they don't, they may find that a cold marriage can be just as chilling as an improperly heated house. Remember that cold marriages don't last very long.

Don and I have been blessed with a plethora of treasured memories as we have served hand in hand in the Lord's kingdom: gospel meetings, lectureships, domestic and foreign mission trips, interacting in the lives of our Christian friends, with both tears and laughter. But we have also taken time for ourselves—walks in the woods, camping trips, anniversary dinners climaxed by listening to the recording of our wedding on the drive home, Valentine dates accented by roses and gifts. Each couple is different, but perhaps the following suggestions may jumpstart your relationship.

- Stay on the lookout for special cards and little gifts for no special occasion. Husbands and wives normally expect gifts from one another on birthdays, Christmases, and even anniversaries. But an occasional little thinking-of-you gift helps to cement a marriage together. Husbands will usually send more cards if we genuinely express our delight and even use them as bookmarks to remind both of us that written words are precious.

It is just as important to regularly set aside money for togetherness as it is to pay the electric bill.

- Feed the children supper early once a week or let them eat in front of the TV so you and your husband can have dinner alone and time to talk.

- Kiss, hold hands, or hug in the presence of your children. Not only is it important to your relationship, it also helps the youngsters feel secure in the knowledge that their mother and daddy love each other.

✳ Look for opportunities to give your husband one sincere compliment each day. Examples:

> "You look great!"
> "I could hardly wait for you to get home."
> "I appreciate the way you have provided for our
>   family."
> "You're the best friend I have."
> "I'm glad I married you."

✳ In your husband's presence, tell other people about his accomplishments.

A wife should be her husband's chief cheerleader, because the ability to give praise is one of the primary qualities a man subconsciously seeks in a woman. Whereas a woman predominantly needs outward signs of affection, he needs your admiration. The benefits of praising your husband and making him feel special are twofold. First, the practice will help you develop the habit of looking for his good traits. It is amazing how many you can find. Second, the activity is reciprocal. He will become much more complimentary of you. It's a win-win situation.

What Children Remember

Each day brings so many opportunities for the making of memories. As parents, we should become aware of their potentialities and actively guide our children through them. From our childhood, all of us remember some of the happenings of everyday life while forgetting many other events. The following situations, however, seem to be the fertile soil for the making of lasting memories for most people. Day by day our children see us—both in our good moods as well as in our bad ones. They watch and they learn.

✳ *Children remember what they hear and see.* Twenty-four hours a day, seven days a week, our children watch the saga of our family as it is acted out on the stage of life. They see us in our angry, frustrated moments as well as in our loving and caring ones. Our words penetrate their hearts and are remembered long after we are gone.

Some parents seem to have only negative remarks to say to their children:

> "You never do anything right."
> "You're the messiest kid I know."
> "You're clumsy."
> "Are you too dense to understand what I said?"

✠ *Children are not mature enough to discern truth from lies.* If they are consistently told how dumb or how clumsy they are, their subconscious minds file such remarks away as the truth and the words later become self-fulfilling prophecies. Fortunate is the child who hears encouraging words from his parents:

> "That was a good job."
> "Nice job on your homework."
> "You are so thoughtful."
> "We love you."
> "You may not have done so well today, but the next time you'll do better."
> "I like the polite way you talked to that older person. It must have made her very happy."

✠ *Children not only remember the words that were said to them, but they also remember the overall tone of the home.* Is it one of peace, harmony, and encouragement? Or does the child constantly hear bickering, fighting, and yelling on the part of the parents and other siblings? Do they hear you telling them one thing and then doing something different?

A child listens, watches, and remembers.

Children Remember Important People

God intended for homes to have fathers who lovingly shoulder the leadership of the home. They should have enough backbone to lead by example and also by guidelines. Not only should good daddies guide, they also should take the time to be a vital part of their children's lives. They should take trips with their families, include their children in some of their hobbies, share household chores, and pitch ball in the backyard before supper. Little boys watch the way their daddies treat their mothers. In all likelihood, they will treat their own wives in the same manner. Children also hear sermons and then they both listen and watch to see whether or not those words make a difference in their daddies' lives.

Children remember their mothers, perhaps best of all. A mother is the hub of the home, managing it so it can function smoothly and each family member can achieve his fullest potential. Children remember freshly baked cookies and family picnics. They will always treasure mom's goodnight kiss and hug at bedtime. They remember her being there when they came home from school and having enough time to sit and listen to reports of all the activities of the day.

Children remember their grandparents, who provide a bridge between the totally different world of parents and children. Because the grandparents no longer have the full responsibility of rearing children—grandchildren can be sent home after a few hours—they usually have more quality time to devote to them than they did to their own children. The pace is a little slower now, allowing for more spontaneous moments. The passing of time reveals many truths. Grandparents have found that some things they demanded of their own children are just not that important. Time is a harsh teacher, but she teaches her lessons well. Consequently, grandparents seem to find more time for fun things with their grandchildren.

Quite often significant people in children's lives are outside the immediate family. Perhaps a favorite aunt or uncle helped them expand their horizons and try their wings. Or it could have been a treasured teacher in school or in a Bible class. I earlier mentioned a Bible teacher who made a difference in my life. Before the days of beautiful visual aids, this teacher could make the characters step out of the Scriptures and become real to us. I caught her attitude and learned to love to study God's Word.

Sadly enough, some people forever remain stamped on children's hearts because of their cruelty. Such people can scar young ones for life. May we resolve to always be a blessing instead of a curse to our children.

Traditions give a family a sense of identity, a sense of belonging.

Children Remember Family Traditions

Young parents are wise when they are aware of the power of traditions and purposefully plan to make treasured memories for their families. Traditions give a family a sense of identity, a sense of belonging. Birthdays are important. The celebration need not be extravagant, but children should be aware that their births are blessings to their families. Some families make videos of their children's birthdays from the time they get out of bed until they are tucked in at the close of the day. Each new birthday is a meaningful time to view the pictures of past birthdays and reflect upon the changes that have transpired through the years.

Thanksgiving is an occasion for families to gather. Each family has its own way of celebrating this holiday, but it is an ideal time for each one sitting around the table to express his or her thankfulness for a significant blessing in his life. It is also an excellent opportunity for older generations to share their earlier ways of observing Thanksgiving.

Christmas holidays are full of opportunities for establishing family traditions. Each family seems to develop its own time for putting up the tree, opening presents, and eating together. The important thing to remember is that it is a time for families to be together and enjoy one another. Because a new marriage brings the merging of two families' traditions, conflicts often arise. Wise parents back off and let the new family unit make its own decisions for the way it wants to handle this holiday.

Ordinary days are rich in opportunities for families to make simple traditions. Wise is the family that takes time to share the evening meal with an exchange of happy events of the day.

Children Remember Childhood Stories

Each of us can easily remember stories. Christ capitalized on the power of a story when He taught eternal truths in the form of parables.

Fortunate is the child who has early memories of bedtime stories being read to her while sitting in the lap of her father or mother. I can remember the bedtime stories my daddy read to me, both fictional and biblical ones.

Blessed is the child whose parents have the originality to make up their own stories. How well I can remember an aunt who used to delight me with her made-up ghost stories. Sometimes children delight in being able to make up their own endings to stories that adults start.

Family stories can become a real legacy. Younger generations need to know what life was like when their parents and grandparents were young. Such tales reveal a family's beliefs and values, as well as their strengths and weaknesses. Over and over in my childhood I heard my daddy tell of his adventures when, as a rebellious teenager, he ran away from home. Again and again he instilled in me the importance of staying in school and getting a good education.

A number of years ago I compiled an aunt's research with my own in tracing our family tree back for thirty-four generations. In the front of the book I made for each of our children, I told them that sometimes we have to know where we have come from before we can know where we are going.

One of our granddaughters often makes a request when we are together. She will pull up a chair and then say, "Grandmother, let's talk about what it was like when you were a little girl." She never seems to tire of the stories that are told over and over.

Children remember Bible stories. Rich is the legacy of a child whose parents lovingly told those eternal stories over and over. Even more blessed is the child whose parents go the second mile by instilling those stories through many different audio-visual aids. It has been said that the Bible is God's diary of the way He has dealt with His people through the years. What unforgettable stories are found within those pages.

Children Remember Milestones

In some cultures children come of age into the adult world by one decisive step, but in our society we seem to cut the apron strings one thread at a time. Records of birthdays are important because each one is a step toward adulthood. The first day of school signals that the child's world is expanding. Losing the first tooth is a sign of growing up. Spending the night away from home with friends, as well as taking trips with them, is a leap toward independence. Summer youth camps and retreats further enable young people to stand on their own two feet. Obtaining the coveted driver's license opens the door to independence. The first job is also significant, as well as the first crush and the first date. Baptism into Christ is the most important milestone of all because it signals spiritual maturity. Children remember all these milestones, including the adults who were there and the surrounding circumstances.

Younger generations need to know what life was like when their parents and grandparents were young.

Children Remember the Rules of Home

No structure can survive without durable framework. Rules and guidelines constitute the framework of the home. Children may not always obey them, but they are never forgotten.

Durable rules have two things in common. First, they are fair. The consequences should fit the crime. Second, they are enforced consistently. Both are challenging, but probably the second one is more difficult.

It is not too hard to establish guidelines that are fair, but being consistent in enforcing them is another question. How many times do parents threaten: "If you do that one more time, I'm going to punish you!" The child then tests his parents by repeating his disobedience, only to hear the same hollow ultimatum given once again. Because he remembers that he previously escaped punishment, he is more confident than ever to disobey.

It is not too hard to establish fair guidelines; but being consistent in enforcing them is another question.

However, if the child understands the rules and is disciplined consistently in a fair manner, he will remember both the rules and the consequences the next time he is tempted to disobey.

Probably the most lasting impression is stamped on a child's mind when he knows what the rules are and is highly praised for following them. We all tend to repeat things that are pleasurable. Good habits are made when correct behavior is repeated until it becomes second nature.

Children Remember the Family Handling Problems

Everyone has adversities, even faithful Christians. They have been promised by God and are the common lot of mankind. If they are handled in the right manner, they can be stepping-stones to growth as we exercise our spiritual muscles and learn to rely upon God and apply His principles to our lives. Figuratively speaking, a person receives a new set of glasses when she becomes a Christian. She encounters problems just like everyone else, but she sees them in a different light. Her new lenses give her a more mature perspective to help her navigate the storms of life.

❊ *Death.* Children are going to watch the way we handle the death of a family member. Do we rant and rave because God failed to grant our prayers the way we wanted them answered? How do we handle criticism? How do we react when we suffer financial losses? The children may be young and we may think they are not fully aware of what is happening. But they do hear. They see. They hurt.

What a blessing it is when young children can see a family pull together as a unit whenever adversity strikes. They learn that it is all right to cry. It is healing to admit our frustration. Children need to know that there will not always be a clear-cut way to handle problems. But they also need to realize that all the family members are there for one another and that their trust is in God to help them reach solutions.

❊ *Peer Pressure.* Children have their own problems, problems that seem unimportant to adults but very important to a youngster. As a former schoolteacher, I am fully aware that being the new student in class can be a terrifying experience. Most parents have never faced the problems young people face today: drugs, violence, premarital sex, alcohol, and lack of moral convictions. Children want to be accepted by their peers, making it tough to make a stand for what is right.

Children will remember parents who made it easy for them to talk about the problems they faced. They will never forget parents who gave them some guidelines ahead of time. "If you are with a group of young people and drugs or alcohol are being used, call home immediately. We will be there in a few minutes." Even before a child is old enough to date, a wise mother and daddy will be specific about what parts of the body can be touched. The child should automatically know that the only clothing that should be removed on a date is a jacket.

✠ *Disappointment and Mistakes.* When young people face disappointments, they need to know that the family is there for them. Perhaps they lost an election for an office at school. Maybe they didn't make the team or they failed to get a part in the school play. Wise parents teach their children that it is all right to stick their necks out and try new things. Some of them work out and some don't. That's life. You can't score points if you're not in the game. But young people need to know that mom and dad are there for them when they hurt.

Just like adults, children make mistakes. How comforting it is to feel the healing balm of forgiveness at home. Parents should encourage them to adopt a "next time" philosophy instead of "if only" one. The past can't be changed but it can be a powerful teacher. Fortunate is the child who is taught to view a mistake as an action that won't work and to look for a new approach. All children will remember adults who helped them through a crisis.

Children Remember Our Walk and Our Talk

It may be fairly easy to lay down guidelines and tell our children what is right and wrong. The difficult part is practicing what we preach. Children hear and witness everything that goes on in the home. They know. And hypocritical parents can easily turn them away from God. Children watch what we do in the kitchen. When we make a casserole for our family, do they see us making an extra one for the family whose mother is in the hospital? Do they see us fixing a fruit basket of cheer for a shut-in? Most important, do they see us going about the task with a happiness that says, "I enjoy doing things for other people because, in essence, I am doing it for the Lord" (Matthew 25:40).

It was Henry Ward Beecher who said, "A helping word to one in trouble is often like a switch on a railroad track . . . An inch between wreck and smooth rolling prosperity." Our helping words or deeds can mean the difference between a smooth trip or a disastrous wreck, not only for those we try to help but also for our own children.

Conclusion

As women, we have been given the primary task of quilting the fabric of our homes. We are responsible, more than any other member of the family, for visualizing the pattern and stitching together the everyday events of life.

All too often we become so caught up in the running of a home that we neglect our husbands. Wise is the wife who realizes that she and her husband need to devote time to one another in making treasured memories of their relationship.

Children may forget many days of their childhood, but there are certain things that will always remain locked in their hearts. Parents need to take the time to learn their importance and then take action to insure the cultivation of positive memories.

Our helping words can mean the difference between a smooth trip or a disastrous wreck . . . for our own children.

Questions for Thought

1. Using verses 13, 19, 21, 22, and 24 of Proverbs 31, describe the skills that the virtuous woman needed to keep her family clothed and warm.

2. Why are patterns needed? Use Exodus 25–27 in giving a report on the divine pattern given for the tabernacle.

3. Describe the legacy of making quilts.

4. In what way are we women the quilt makers of our homes?

5. Do you agree or disagree with the statement that the most valuable legacy we can leave our children is the gift of memories? Why?

6. What would a quilt be like without a pattern? What is your pattern for the quilt of your home?

7. What are some factors that can later destroy the closeness a husband and wife share at the time of their wedding?

8. Discuss the four suggestions made in the lesson regarding restoring the closeness in the marriage union. Add your own.

9. What are some derogatory remarks that can undermine a child's sense of his worth? Do we really mean what we say in such remarks?

10. What is there about the overall tone of the home that a child remembers?

11. Discuss the important people in a child's life and the impact they have upon his development.

12. Why do you think family traditions are important?

13. Children remember the stories they hear throughout childhood. Discuss the impact of the following kinds of stories and add your own suggestions—bedtime stories, made-up stories, family stories, and Bible stories.

14. Children remember the rules of home. Durable guidelines have what two characteristics in common? Which one is more difficult to enforce?

15. What actions do we usually tend to repeat, the ones that were rigidly enforced or the ones that brought us pleasure?

16. Children remember the manner in which their families handled problems. If God really loves us, why do we have problems?

17. Discuss some problems that children normally encounter. How can we parents be of help to them?

18. How can we help a child deal with his mistakes?

19. Why is it sometimes difficult for our walk to match our talk? What can we do about it?

Anniversary cruise, 2006

St. Simon's Island 1997, 2nd honeymoon, same hotel as 1956

Marriage is not made in heaven. It comes in a kit and has to be put together.

Don and Jane in Ireland, 1999

Getting Specific:
How to Make and Preserve
Memories

So far in this study we have discussed the importance of memories as well as creating an awareness of the potential of the everyday moments of life. In this chapter we are going to be specific in giving examples of ways to seize the moment and capture its treasures.

Preserved by God

From the days of Noah, visual reminders have been vital in remembering significant events. "The rainbow shall be in the cloud, and I will look on it to remember the everlasting covenant between God and every living creature of all flesh that is on the earth" (Genesis 9:16).

Each year the Jews gathered in their homes to remember that night in Egypt when the Lord passed over the houses of the Israelites where the blood of sacrificial lambs had been sprinkled. Once again they ate the roasted meat, unleavened bread, and bitter herbs. This annual reenactment with all the visual reminders preserved the memory of God's deliverance.

God's commandments to His people, written on stone, were to be preserved in the ark of the covenant as a constant reminder of the covenant between Jehovah and the Israelites (Hebrews 9:4).

God's commandments to His people, written on stone, were to be preserved in the ark of the covenant.

When the Israelites rebelled against God's appointed leaders, the Almighty settled the matter by commanding each tribe to submit a rod with the leader's name. All twelve rods were placed in the tabernacle to await the sign of God's approval. Only the rod of Aaron—for the house of Levi—budded. Not only did it bud, it also produced blossoms and even almonds. Aaron's rod was kept in the ark of the covenant as a tangible reminder of God's will in the selection of leadership (Numbers 17; Hebrews 9:4).

When God's people were led out of bondage, something had to be done for nourishment for that nation of people who were wandering in a desert. The manna, miraculously sent, may not have been gourmet food, but it prevented starvation. Israel's realization that an actual pot of manna was preserved in the ark of the covenant was a reminder of God's care of His people (Exodus 16:31–34; Hebrews 9:4).

Every time the Israelites changed locations, the ark of the covenant was moved with them. Although they were not permitted to look inside the ark, it was a constant reminder of the Ten Commandments, Aaron's rod that budded, and the pot of manna.

The death of Christ was the ultimate sacrifice for the sins of mankind. Simply telling the story of His crucifixion from time to time would not have been enough to keep that memory alive through the ages. In His wisdom Christ instituted the Lord's supper on the night He was betrayed with the bread representing His body and the fruit of the vine representing His blood (Matthew 26:26–28). Throughout future generations His followers would have a reminder of His sacrifice every first day of the week, as they partake of these tangible emblems (Acts 20:7).

Making Memories

Some of the following suggestions are ideas I have tried and have found to be successful. Others are concepts that I either read or learned from friends and wish that I had used when our children were still at home. They are intended only to be used as jumper cables to get your own minds started in the right direction. The last part of the chapter deals with specific ways to preserve your memories.

Specific "Making Memories" Guidelines

Some, but not all, of our special moments just happen. Many of them are already there, waiting for us to realize their values, but the potentiality of so many others lies dormant until we purposefully decide to make family memories. Perhaps the following suggestions will help.

1. *Take one of the children out to eat, to a movie, or to some other event he will enjoy, while Dad and the other children stay at home.* It is an excellent time to develop one-on-one quality time with the children.

   One of my fondest childhood memories was the time my mother and I dressed in our Sunday best and rode the city bus into Nashville when I was about six years old to have lunch in the dining room of the Hermitage Hotel, complete with white tablecloths, fresh flowers, and live music. I loved it!

2. Leave an occasional surprise—a piece of candy, a book—on each of your children's pillows, along with a note of encouragement.

3. Make the end of the day a time to remember with bedtime stories, including Bible stories, and prayers for younger children. Both younger and older children should always get a goodnight kiss and a hug, in addition to free time to "just talk."

4. Purchase some sets of flannel graph and other aids for teaching Bible stories in family devotionals. Invest in books that give suggestions for object lessons. Use workbooks. When our children were young, for a period of time we daily stretched a string between two chairs to hold cards representing each Bible story we had studied. Periodically we mixed them up and let the children put them in order to help them gain a perspective of chronology.

5. Have a family meeting in the kitchen and bake cookies. Children will always remember the aroma of cookies they have had a hand in baking. When the cookies are finished, take your children with you to deliver them to some shut-ins, those at home as well as the ones in a nursing home.

6. Use your kitchen table for making cards to send to shut-ins and those who are in the hospital.

7. Encourage your children to plant and cultivate flower seeds in decorated pots. When the plants have matured sufficiently, your children can help you take them to some shut-ins.

8. Help your children develop patience by counting down to a special occasion. Use either a chalkboard or a calendar-like device in which the pages can be torn off with each passing day. Count down the days to an exciting event: vacation time, a visit from the grandparents, or a holiday.

9. *Have an impromptu picnic on a sunny day with such simple things as peanut butter and jelly sandwiches.* On cold, rainy winter days, have a picnic in front of the fireplace.

10. *Have a Family Fun Night once a month with games, popcorn, and no television.*

11. *Take a walk with your children, noticing the flowers, animals, and bugs along the way.*

12. *View both a sunrise and a sunset with your family.* Nothing can surpass the beauty of this act of nature.

13. *Sing regularly together.* Families who sing together, at home or in the car, develop a strong bond.

14. *Plan family reunions so the younger generation can connect with the older one.* Have each person tell one important thing that has happened since the last reunion.

15. *Allow your children to make tents on special days inside the house out of old blankets and sheets.* Let them sleep there that night.

16. *Wake up the birthday child with a "Happy Birthday" song.* Make a video of the day from the first waking moment until the lights are turned out that night.

17. *Make a tree house for the children and allow them to have special time there alone.* I thoroughly enjoyed the one my daddy built for me.

Take your children with you to deliver cookies to shut-ins.

18. *Help your children with special projects.* One of the best memories of my childhood was the doll house I made from cardboard boxes. I painted them on the outside, cut holes for windows, made curtains, papered the walls with samples of wallpaper from the paint store, cut rugs from the Sears catalog, and pasted them on the floor. When

I had saved enough from my allowance (25 cents a week), I bought plastic furniture (a piece at a time) to furnish the house. I was so proud of it!

19. *Keep a store-bought roll of cookies in the refrigerator for impromptu treats.*

20. *Make it a habit to hug and kiss your family members before going your separate ways each day.*

21. *Let your youngsters enjoy the love of their own animal, if that is feasible.* I'll never forget the dog I had from the time I was five years old until my college days. I also had a pet duck for many years. One year my parents gave me two rabbits. You guessed it! It wasn't long until my daddy had to build a hutch for the rabbits' expanding family.

22. *Join hands while offering thanks at mealtime.* At dinner take time for each person to tell something good about his or her day.

23. *Encourage your husband to include the children in his hobbies.* When our son was twelve, Don began taking him hunting. They also shared in the hobby of photography, both the making and the developing of pictures. Mothers need to include their daughters in some of their favorite pastimes—like shopping!

24. *Use a special plate at mealtime for a child when it is his birthday or when some other milestone—making the honor roll or the team—has been achieved.* Plates with "special day" inscriptions can be purchased, or an inexpensive colorful plastic plate can be bought. The main idea is that the plate is special and the child is special on that day.

25. *Designate a special time, at least once a year, for the family to gather around the kitchen table with hot chocolate and their favorite dessert.* Mom, Dad, and children bring a paper with their thoughts on what their family means to them, complete with drawings. After the papers have been shared with the family, place them in a special scrapbook to become a treasure chest of family memories.

26. *Cook each child's favorite meal at least once a month.*

27. *Start a charm bracelet for your young daughter, adding special charms for each milestone of her life.*

28. *Let the children make Christmas tree ornaments.* Kits of wooden figures to be painted are available as well as felt ones to be glued and decorated.

29. *Make ornaments with current pictures of your children each Christmas.* As the years go by, they become a chronicle of the way the family has looked through the years.

> *When the family gathers around the table at Thanksgiving, let each person tell about one thing for which he is thankful.*

30. *Set a time for thankful expressions.* For example, when the family gathers around the table at Thanksgiving, let each person tell about one thing for which he is thankful.

31. *Make a Thanksgiving tablecloth.* The November 2003 issue of *Ladies' Home Journal* (p. 86) featured an article about this practice. Using a different colored permanent marker each year, let each person write what he has been thankful for during that year and sign the note. As inscriptions are added each year in different colors, the tablecloth becomes a legacy.

32. *Cut patterns from the scraps of your family's clothing to be made later into a quilt.*

33. *Have a meeting at the beginning of the year and designate one weekend during that year for each of your children to select some activity (within reason) for the family to do together.*

34. *Pack notes from you in your family's lunchboxes from time to time.*

35. *Gather the family to decorate eggs to be hidden at an Easter egg hunt.*

36. *Hang a bulletin board in the kitchen for all family members to share upcoming activities and accomplishments.*

37. *Look for ways to familiarize your children with old family friends.* For example, during the month of December, at supper time read aloud the cards that arrived in the mail that day. It's a good opportunity for the younger children to learn about some important people who now live far away.

38. *Set aside about thirty minutes with you children for after-school snacks and general conversation before they plunge into home-work, chores, or other activities.* Listen to them! One of my favorite memories is that of my mother sitting at a table by the kitchen window with a cup of coffee while waiting for me to walk home from school. We always had time to talk about what happened that day.

39. *Take the family camping.* Nothing bonds a family quite like camping, with meals cooked over a fire and walks in the woods.

40. *As the children mature, designate one evening a month for each older child to prepare dinner for the family.* This practice lays a good foundation for skills that will be needed throughout life. Let them plan the menu and have all the ingredients there for them to use.

Preserving Memories

Potential memories are all around us, just waiting to be noticed. Equally as important as becoming aware of their potentiality is the need for preserving them. We think we will never forget, but we do. Most of the time, all that is needed is a reminder and the treasured memory floats back as if it had just happened today.

There are many ways to preserve yesterday's moments so they can always be with us. The remainder of this chapter suggests some. Hopefully, they will generate your thinking and help you find new ways to prevent those events from slipping away.

1. *Utilize the refrigerator door.* That is perhaps the most obvious way to preserve memories. For decades that essential piece of kitchen equipment has doubled its usefulness by also serving as a showcase for a family's life.

2. *Make a memory book.* "Scrapbooking" has become an art in more recent years. With the newer albums, no longer are pictures just "put" in an album. We have learned how to decorate each page and add notes of our own.

   As mentioned earlier in this book, I found a treasure of family snapshots when going through my daddy's possessions after he died. At that time I resolved not only to straighten out my parents' keepsakes but also to go through all those pictures and mementos—such as report cards and letters—of our own family and do something with them. To the best of my ability I dated and identified every picture, along with the other mementos, divided them equally, and made several scrapbooks for each of our children.

3. *Involve the family in making a "summer scrapbook" using pictures and keepsakes from all their summer activities.* Each summer add to it. It is also a good idea to make a separate

booklet for each trip the family takes so the happy events can be remembered from time to time.

4. *Create a "life experience" book.* Schoolteachers know the value of such a project. Nothing stimulates a child's interest in reading quite like reading an account of something he has done. The next time there is some special event—whether you're visiting your grandchildren, they are visiting you, or your own children are doing something noteworthy—make a roll of pictures and use your computer to write a few comments to go on each page along with a picture. Staple the pages together or put them in a binder and you have a booklet of memories.

5. *Create "first day of school" pictures by photographing each child on the first day of school standing at your front door or some other place of interest.* Compile a little album of the first-day-of-school pictures for each child and present it to them when they are grown.

6. *Buy a decorative yardstick for each child's room and mark his height on each birthday, along with a picture made at that time.* Our son and his wife have been remodeling a house built in 1925. There was one area, however, over which they didn't have the heart to paint. The previous owners had used the inside of a closet door in one of the bathrooms to mark the height of their children, along with each one's name. The first entry was in 1932 and the last one was in the 1950s. This door had been very special to that family. What a collection of memories!

7. *Write a letter to your child on his birthday, but don't tell him.* Emphasize some of the major events that occurred during the previous year, as well as how much he means to you. Include two or three significant photographs. Seal the envelopes and give them to him when he is grown.

8. *Frame mementos of special milestones in your children's lives—favorite baby outfit, baby shoes, and football shirts.* When your child or grandchild is in a special program at school, frame the program, along with a few snapshots of the child as he appeared at that event.

9. *Install shelves to hold sentimental objects that are too large to frame.* As I mentioned earlier, on one of our den walls is a shelf with my daddy's red fire engine that he played with as a little boy, along with his cap pistol. That shelf is surrounded by pictures made during the various phases of his life.

10. *Turn your cookbook into a memory saver.* I never recopy recipes. Wherever I am when I find a good recipe, I write it on whatever piece of paper is available, along with the cook's name. My cookbooks contain some recipes written on napkins and even paper plates. Each time I use them, I think of the person who gave me that recipe and also the place where we ate.

11. *Think of your journal as a treasure chest.* I kept diaries all through elementary school, high school, and college. Looking back over them now brings back a flood of memories. Recently I pulled those diaries out of the drawer and reread them. A few of the recorded events are a complete blank to me now. But the trigger of just a few words makes most of those days just as vivid as if they had happened only yesterday—giving my dog a bath in a washtub in the back yard and letting my pet duck swim in the water, slumber parties, ball

> *Write a letter to your child on his birthday, but don't tell him. Seal the envelope and give it to him when he is grown.*

games, having the neighbors over for cookouts in our back yard, joining other teenagers from church in singing for shut-ins, school trips, dorm life at Lipscomb, dating days.

Reading about my childhood and teenage years helped me remember what a blessed life I have had. Sometimes we fail to realize that life is composed of ordinary days, which become ordinary weeks that, in turn, become the ordinary years of our lives. While most of these days, months, and years are not spectacular, they are priceless because they become the building blocks of life, held together by some very special cement. Memories!

Although I no longer keep a daily diary, several years ago I began keeping a journal that I call my "Happy Book." I usually make entries five or six times a month—whenever I want to capture a happy moment to be preserved for years to come. More recently I began taping appropriate snapshots on the pages with the entries. These journals are some of my most prized possessions.

12. *Arrange a special display of family pictures.* When we moved into our present house (with its long, wide hall) a number of years ago, I selected some of the significant pictures of our children's lives from babyhood through college. Then I bought numerous large frames (20 x 24) and some matting. A friend cut the matting to display our various sized pictures from snapshots to 8 x 10 portraits. Each of our two children has a wall. Now walking down the hall is like remembering each child from babyhood through the early adult years.

13. *Tape conversations and correspondence with family members.* Earlier I mentioned the audio tapes that were mailed back and forth between our family and my mother and daddy. Videos are normally made on special occasions, but these audio tapes told of the everyday happenings of the two households. Listening to them periodically always brings back a flood of memories as I once again hear our voices, as well as those of my parents, while we talk about life—everyday life that is so special.

14. *Sit down with your parents and talk about the happenings of their lives.* Earlier I mentioned that I persuaded my daddy to make an audio tape one time when he visited me. We talked about the memories of his childhood, how he met my mother, and all the other important events of his life. His voice was so weak that later the tape had to have special electronic help by a friend to make it audible. Death claimed his life less than five months after the tape was made. Needless to say, it has become one of my most prized possessions.

> *Life is not measured by the years we live, but rather by the moments that take our breath away.*

Conclusion

Life is filled with memories, both those already there and those moments that have the potentiality of becoming treasures of the heart. We need to seize these opportunities before they slip through our fingers. Wise are the parents who search for ways to make family memories. If we are smart, we will do everything possible to preserve these memories to be enjoyed in years to come. It has been said that life is not measured by the years we live but rather by the moments that take our breath away. They are gifts. Guard these treasures wisely.

Questions for Thought

1. How does the Bible reinforce the wisdom of preserving memories?

2. What memorial did God command that involved the sense of taste? What similar memorial do we keep today?

3. What visual reminders were preserved in the ark of the covenant? Why?

4. Why do parents need some personal time with each child? Why is it so difficult to schedule?

5. Discuss the lesson's suggestions for home Bible studies, adding your own pointers.

6. How can cooking together bond family members?

7. Why is it important to include your children with you as you do your acts of service to others?

8. Try having a family night with selected activities and no television. Report your evaluation to the class.

9. What is the value of family reunions?

10. Sharing a good thing that happened to each family member at mealtime helps to bond a family as they interact with one another's lives. It also is fertile soil for what other habit?

11. What is the benefit of including the children in some of the parents' hobbies? What are the drawbacks?

12. Several suggestions were made for developing memories during the Christmas season. Which ones are your favorites?

13. Which Thanksgiving suggestion do you like best for your family?

14. Some children don't seem to open up very well with their parents. What can parents do to foster better communication?

15. Why is camping such an ideal environment for making happy memories?

16. Forty suggestions were given for opportunities to help families make memories. Which one holds the most potential for your family? Which other ones would you suggest?

17. Share with the class the methods of scrapbooking that your family has found to be useful.

18. What is your favorite way to display family pictures?

19. This lesson gave fourteen suggestions for preserving memories. What other ones seem to be the best for your family? Add those to the list.

Don and Jane at Kathy's wedding, 1987

Kathy's wedding (L-R): Don, Tony, Kathy, Jane, Greg

Speaker at Regions University lectureship, 2001

Creating Paper Treasures

The art of writing encouraging notes has almost become a lost art in this day of email and cell phones. However, letters have the magical potential to encourage—not once or twice but as many times as we pull out that faded page and again read those gifts from the soul that transport love and concern from one heart to another. Unlike the irritating ring of the telephone, written words give the recipient a choice of the most ideal time to receive the message. What a blessing it is to curl up by a fire on a cold winter day and read treasured letters!

Most people are repulsed by the idea of writing notes. They mean well, but they're always busy and often don't even have suitable stationery or stamps. One of the most common excuses is the wail: "I just don't know what to say." Because of this need, Peggy Coulter (Publishing Designs, Inc) and I collaborated in writing a study titled *Special Delivery* to offer suggestions for making the task easier, including an in-depth Bible study of each topic.

The written word, once a part of the writer, becomes a part of the recipient to encourage her for many years to come. Throughout our lives, what a blessing it is to leave a paper trail of encouraging words to those around us. Lengthy letters are not required or even desired. Instead, short thoughts from our hearts can become paper treasures to hundreds of people who cross our pathways of life.

The Written Word in the Scriptures

The Ten Commandments

During the early times of God's dealing with mankind, He simply spoke to them. However, when the law was given to Moses on Mount Sinai, the Almighty chose to write His commandments on two tables of stone with His own finger. Later, these commandments were so important that they were put in the ark of the covenant and placed in the most holy place of the tabernacle (Exodus 40:20).

Commandments between the Eyes and on the Doorposts

In Deuteronomy 6:1–8, Moses instructed the Israelites to write an all-encompassing commandment, first of all, in their hearts so they could teach them to their children. God then was explicit in commanding them to take advantage of every opportunity to teach this message to their children: when they sat in their houses, walked by the way, and lay down in bed at night, as well as when they rose up in the morning.

In addition to utilizing the spoken word, the people were told to bind these commandments on their hands and as frontlets between their eyes, as well as writing them on the posts of their homes. Written words were found on the Israelites' hands, between their eyes, and even on their doorposts.

The Book of Psalms

The book of Psalms, a collection of religious poems set to music and used in Jewish public worship, contain some of the nation's most treasured written words. Because David had such deep feelings and was a devoted servant of God, he was a natural selection as the author of so many psalms. However, numerous others were composed by various men.

Written Words Brought Tears

The copying of the law and other parts of the Scriptures was done by men known as the scribes. One of the best known scribes was the priest Ezra (Ezra 7:6–10).

After returning from the Exile, the Israelites asked Ezra the scribe to read the written law to them. They stood from morning until midday while he read God's Word from a pulpit made of wood. "For all the people wept, when they heard the words of the Law" (Nehemiah 8:9). They wept because they had not kept it.

They stood from morning until midday while Ezra read God's word. They wept because they had not kept it.

The second day, when the people learned they were to observe the Feast of Booths, they gathered branches and lived in booths for seven days, something they had not done since the days of Joshua the son of Nun. From the first day of the feast until the last, the words of the law were read to them (Nehemiah 8:18). What a difference the written words made in their lives!

The Epistles

How rich are the words of the epistles—written primarily by Paul—to various congregations of the Lord's people that were scattered throughout the then-known world.

The writers' words brought rebuke, instruction, and encouragement. We can only begin to imagine the excitement as those written words were read to the various assemblies. Because they were written, they could be reread many times.

The book of Revelation contains the letters to the seven churches of Asia, written by John on the Isle of Patmos. Like Paul, John used his letters both to encourage and rebuke.

The Power of the Written Word

The following touching story appeared in my recent book, *Special Delivery.*

At the conclusion of a trying day, a junior high school teacher asked her class to participate in a rather unusual activity. She told them to make a list of everyone in the class and then write something good about each person. After she had collected the assignments, the following weekend she wrote each child's name on a separate piece of paper and compiled a copy of all the good comments made about that particular person, adding her own words to the list. The next Monday she gave each student a copy of all the good things other class members had written about him or her.

The teacher did not think too much about what she had done until a number of years later. One of those students (Mark) was killed in Vietnam. He had been particularly full of himself in her junior high class, in addition to her third grade class several years earlier. Quite frankly, he had tried her patience at times. But she was very fond of him, and they had corresponded during his stint in Vietnam.

After the young man's funeral, his parents showed the teacher something that had been sent home from the war with his other personal belongings. Imagine her surprise when they produced a well worn sheet of paper that had been folded many times and taped together. It was the paper she had given him when he was in her class on that day long ago. Judging from the frayed condition of the page, he undoubtedly had reached for it frequently to reread all the good comments written about him by his fellow students as well as his teacher.

Several classmates also attended Mark's funeral. They began telling their favorite teacher they also had saved their own lists of the good things their fellow students had written about them in math class that day long ago. One had preserved his copy in his wedding album; another had kept her list in her diary; still another one, like Mark, carried his paper in his wallet. How much all of them had treasured those words! Their responses brought tears to the teacher's eyes as she pondered the power of the written word. (*The Birmingham News*, February 7, 1999.)

A Gift of Everyday Kindness

As I mentioned earlier, the bookshelves in our home hold some special treasures: several notebooks containing letters and notes we have received throughout the years. They are not routine correspondence. Sometimes people write letters because it is the proper thing to do. By way of contrast, our notebooks of messages contain gifts from the heart—words that are written just because someone wanted to go the second mile to offer encouragement or say thank you for a special kindness.

We all need notes of encouragement. During difficult times, we often take those notebooks from the shelves and read the letters once again. As we begin, we are reminded of the events that prompted their writing. Each time we browse through these treasures, we can still see the writers' faces, hear their voices, smell the food we enjoyed together, and feel the warmth of their touches or hugs. It has never failed. We always go away with renewed determination to keep on trying because those people have been kind enough to express their feelings by telling us we have made a difference in their lives.

Their responses brought tears to the teacher's eyes as she pondered the power of the written word.

Roses in December

When we were traveling in another state several years ago, I read some words on the wall of a gift shop and the thought impressed me. I don't remember the exact wording but the thrust of the message was: "God gave us memories so we could gather roses in December." The winter of life comes to all of us if we live long enough. How heartwarming and refreshing it is to read through special letters that have become our paper treasures.

At the turn of our new millennium, Gutenberg was selected by a panel as the most influential person of the past thousand years. His invention of the printing press made possible the transfer of ideas from one individual to the masses by means of the printed page. The success of most of the other great people during that period of time would have been impossible without his contribution.

Written words are powerful as they span the ages and touch all classes of people. The printing press influenced millions of people. On a different scale, our own written words—whether they are done by hand or other means—can have an equally important impact upon the hearts of other human beings. These heart gifts convey, in a permanent form, our love and concern. How powerful they are!

Making Preparation

Gather Materials

Certain things are required. A soldier is indeed foolish if he goes into battle without the proper protective clothing, as well as the weapons he will need to fight the enemy. In the same line of thought, a Christian will probably not be successful in making very many paper treasures for people to cherish if she does not keep the needed materials at her fingertips.

Just as God began to execute His plan for the deliverance of the Israelites by using the common staff that shepherds held in their hands on a daily basis, so can He use the common objects in our hands to His glory. However, if we do not have the necessary equipment at our fingertips, we tend to procrastinate until the initial burst of desire has vanished.

Writing Tools

Obviously, the first requirement would be the tools needed to write. A pen and paper are necessary for the making of paper treasures. Neither has to be expensive. Whenever you are in a dollar store, keep your eyes open for attractive greeting cards—usually fifty cents each—as well as blank notes. Designate a drawer for your supplies and keep it well stocked. How many times do we mention that we want to send someone a note, only to discover that we will first have to shop for a card. By the time we fight the traffic and return home, we often have lost our desire. The same is true for stamps. Always keep a supply of the things you will need. If your lifestyle involves sitting in waiting rooms for appointments, tuck a package of note cards in your purse. When pens, paper, and stamps are at hand, using pockets of time wisely becomes a habit.

If we do not have tools at our fingertips, we tend to procrastinate until the burst of desire vanishes.

Awareness—Keen Eyes, Listening Ears

The second requirement is a keen eye and a listening ear. Church bulletins are a rich source of the names of people who need our encouragement. Don't just assume that others will send cards. It is just as much your responsibility as it is theirs.

If you live in a small town, scan your local newspaper for pictures and articles about people who have achieved milestones or who have experienced sorrow. Cut out the article and send it to them with your personal comments.

A network of friends can be very effective in keeping one another informed about both the sorrows and the joys of other people.

A Caring Heart

The third requirement is a caring heart. We normally think about writing to those who are sick or grieving, but other opportunities are limitless. Become a collector of moments suitable for reaching out to people who cross your path. When a salesperson goes out of her way to help you, write the store manager a note commending that clerk. We may think that professional people don't need our thanks, but they do. Write your doctor and preacher and tell them how much you appreciate what they are doing. Write a note to visitors to worship services, encouraging them to return because a warm welcome awaits them. Let your child's schoolteacher know how much you appreciate the long hours she invests in her job and the personal attention she has given to your child. Write a note to your parents, thanking them for their many years of caring for you. Be there with a note for your children during difficult times. Send your husband a heartfelt note to thank him for all he has meant to you through the years.

We normally think about writing to the sick or grieving, but other opportunities are limitless.

The world is full of opportunities to make paper treasures for other people if we will only keep the right tools on hand, open our eyes and ears, and keep our hearts tender.

Opportunities

For years I have looked at a quotation I copied in the front of my Bible. "The days come and go, but they say nothing. If we do not use the gifts they bring, they carry them as silently away"

(Emerson). The dawn of each new day brings its own gifts—the opportunities to make a difference in the lives of others. If we are too busy to even be aware of those precious moments, they will be carried away silently at the close of day, nevermore to return. How wise is the person who is aware of the following opportunities. (A suggested note, taken from my book, *Special Delivery*, is given in each category to jump start your own batteries.)

Remember the rules of successful note writing: short, sincere, specific, and spontaneous.

Gift

I was truly touched by your "gift of the heart." The holiday towel makes the house look festive. I appreciate your thoughtfulness more than words can express. Thanks so much not only for your act of kindness on this occasion but also for all you do for others throughout the year.

Hospitality

Words cannot begin to express how much we enjoyed being in your home recently. Everything conveyed the message of your love and concern. From the moment we stepped through the door, we knew we were in a special place. Your hospitality seemed to wrap its arms around us and made us feel loved. Thank you for seeing that all our needs were met in such a warm, relaxing manner. We will never forget our time spent with you.

Act of Kindness

The mountain of dirty clothes was beginning to pile up, and I was wondering what I would do until I recovered from my bout with the flu. Like a little fairy, you popped in the door one day. You didn't say, "Is there anything I can do for you?" Instead, you said, "I've come to wash your clothes." What a blessing that was! You have been by my side through thick and thin for many years now.

Thank you not only for doing the laundry but also for being my friend.

Preacher

Your sermon this morning was powerful! In addition to being biblically sound, the lesson was filled with applications to my own life. You have such a gifted way of communicating your thoughts to others. Yet, in addition to your natural abilities, I am aware that many hours of preparation are required to present a lesson effectively. Thank you for all your efforts. We appreciate you.

Elders

Most of us fail to realize the many hours you elders invest in fulfilling your responsibilities. We appreciate your study of the Scriptures and your watchful care of the spiritual diet of the flock. Lest you think we take you for granted, I wanted to put my heartfelt thanks on paper to remind you that you are loved and appreciated.

New Convert

Welcome to God's family of believers! Your baptism made many people happy, and we know there was joy in heaven. Your fellow Christians love you and want to be of help. I would like for you to attend Bible class with me on Sunday morning and have dinner with my family after the worship services. I'll give you a call to confirm the arrangements.

Former Bible Teacher

My mature years have caused me to realize what a tremendous influence you had on me during my early childhood. I simply want to say thank you for the impact of your Bible classes. Throughout the years I have been blessed with many wonderful teachers, and I have learned much about the Bible in their classes. But the time spent with you took me one step further. You taught me to want to study the Scriptures for myself. Probably the word "taught" is the wrong word. Actually I "caught" your love of Bible study. (Usually attitudes are "caught" better than they are "taught.") I will forever be grateful for the difference you have made in my life.

Food Preparer

How very much like you to always be thinking of other people! We wish you could have been hiding behind the door and could have seen how much we enjoyed your chicken casserole. Oh, was it delicious! All we had to add was a salad and we had a meal. Thanks for loving us and for showing that love in such a meaningful way.

Mom

Mom, thank you for always being there for me. Not for one minute have I ever doubted your love. I always felt that I was wanted and cherished. Many children in today's world can't say that. One of the most important things you ever did for me was to teach me to believe in myself. Because of you, I learned it's all right to stick my neck out and try new things. Thank you for giving me that confidence.

Dad

All too often I fail to stop and thank you for being such a wonderful dad. You had time to do things with me, whether it was helping me study spelling words, building pens for my pets, or hanging a swing from the big tree in the yard. You were always there, and I knew I could count on you. Thank you for all you mean to me.

Husband

Thank you for always being there whenever I have needed someone to turn to. Thank you for your patience in putting up with me. Thank you for loving me even when I am unlovable. Thank you for your thoughtfulness in expressing your love for me by numerous beautiful gifts and so many meaningful words all through the years.

Child

We could not begin to put into the words of one letter just how much you have meant to us through the years. We know of many good, conscientious parents who have tried hard and yet have had children who have been disappointments. You have been such a blessing to our lives, and we have always been so proud of you in many ways, especially because of what you are on the inside. We are thankful for your strength of character and, most of all, your love for God. We are proud to be your parents. We love you with all our hearts. Don't ever forget how much you mean to us.

Friend

I see the countless things you do, so many good things. I see the struggle in your life, the bravery in your smile. I see your love and kindness dispensed with ease and grace. I see the wondrous love of God reflected in your face. I am blessed to have you as my friend.

Bride and Groom

My heart joins with many other friends in wishing you the very best on your wedding day. For quite some time, I have watched your love for one another blossom. My love and best wishes will go with you as you begin your journey of life together.

Graduate

Congratulations on your achievement! All your years of diligent study have finally paid off. You have mastered many tools for living; now the time has come to put them to good use. Those tools will be of little value unless you have a direction in life. Set your goals reasonably high. If you don't quite make them, you will undoubtedly achieve more in life than if you had never taken aim. Our love and best wishes will go with you. We have been proud of you for many years now and anticipate hearing great things about you in the future. We will be behind you every step of the way.

Career Advancement

Quite some time ago I knew it was only a matter of time until all your hard work and ability would be rewarded with a promotion. Congratulations! You are certainly worthy of this honor because your skills make you an asset to any company. My best wishes go with you in your new work. I am confident your future holds many more such promotions.

Loss of Loved One

My deepest sympathy goes out to you. We become so deeply entwined with those whom we love that it seems as if part of our flesh has been ripped away when they leave us. In my own life I have found that the wounds of grief will heal with the passing of time if they are treated properly. I pray the day will come when thoughts of your loved one will seem as refreshing as a soft breeze on a spring day. May you then think of him and smile instead of crying. But, at this moment, you ache and thoughts of your beloved only bring tears. I feel helpless and wish I could do something to help you with your grief. Remember that I love you.

Illness

I was so sorry to learn of your illness and just want to let you know you are in my thoughts and prayers. Lying in bed can be quite trying, but I pray your sickness will prove to be a blessing in disguise. An illness pulls us out of the rat race of human existence and allows time for introspection. Just as the rests in a musical score are as important as the notes that are played, so can the rests in our lives be as beneficial as all our frenzied activities. If you look back over the melody of your own life, undoubtedly you can understand how beautiful the rests have been. It has been said that for health and wealth to be appreciated, they must first be interrupted. We all tend to take good health for granted when we are well. My prayers are with you as you recover.

Divorce

You have been wounded and the future must seem uncertain and even a bit frightening for you. Remember that I am here for you, only a phone call away. You remain in my daily prayers.

Parents of Wayward Child

In your eyes I have seen the sorrow caused by your son's actions. I have also observed the way you reared him. No child has ever had better parents. Remember that each person must stand on his own two feet and be accountable for his own actions. Your child made some wrong choices, but we pray the Word you helped plant in his heart will bring him to his senses one day. Our love and prayers are with you. Whenever you feel the need to talk to someone, please call. I am here for you.

Conclusion

The potential list of examples of the power of the written word is limitless. The samples taken from *Special Delivery* are cited in this chapter to help you begin thinking of ways you can make paper treasures for your families, friends, co-workers, and fellow Christians. I will close this chapter with a story that powerfully depicts the effects of a few written words. It appeared in the February 20, 2002, issue of our newspaper in Fayette, Alabama, *The Times Record*. Because it touched my heart, I also quoted it in *Special Delivery*.

> Once upon a time there was a little old lady who lived alone on the side of a country road. Her days were long and lonely and many times the only person passing to speak was the rural mail carrier.
> Faithfully she sat in her old porch swing and waited patiently— even hopefully—for him. Even though she never received a letter, she'd

wave cheerfully and call out a friendly greeting, which he always re-
turned. Then she's go inside—for the excitement and expectancy of
the day was past. However, bright and early the next morning, she
would return to her porch, regardless of the weather to wait again.
Years passed and the postman retired. Looking back over his time of
service and recalling patrons and incidents, he realized how much she
had meant to him. Many times her cheerful greetings had brightened
his day and made him more appreciative of his ability to work, to
serve, and to travel along the lovely countryside to see people
and mix and mingle with them. She had taught a great
lesson in patience as she waited endlessly for a letter
which never came. Considering how truly important
she had been to him, he decided to write her a letter
of thanks.

> *His letter*
> *was found*
> *in her apron*
> *pocket . . . the*
> *edges were*
> *frayed and*
> *worn and it*
> *was stained.*

   Some time later her body was found in the
little house by the side of the road. She had died
all alone. His letter was found in her apron pock-
et. Its edges were frayed and worn and it was
stained. Evidently she had read it over and over
again and again, feeding on the joy and comfort
the few kind words had offered to her weary and
lonely heart.

May this chapter help you realize the
power of paper treasures. All of us can make
them if only we will realize their importance
and take the necessary time.

Questions for Thought

1. Why has the writing of notes almost become a lost art?

2. Describe God's first writing to man.

3. What instructions does Deuteronomy 6 give for getting the
   written Word of God before the people on a daily basis?

4. Using a Bible reference book, research the use of psalms in
   temple worship.

5. When the Jews returned from exile, they asked Ezra to read the written law to them. Under what conditions was it read? (Nehemiah 8:1–8). The power of those written words caused what kind of reaction? (Nehemiah 8:9–18).

6. Discuss the impact of the epistles upon the early church.

7. Have you kept any letters or notes? Why are they so special?

8. Why was Gutenberg selected as the most influential person of the past millennium?

9. Discuss the three requirements needed for making paper treasures.

10. Twenty areas of opportunities for the creation of paper treasures were listed. After reading them, select three of the categories and write your own notes.

11. This chapter concluded with a story about a lonely elderly woman who treasured a note written to her by her mail carrier. Discuss people in your community who may fall into that category. What can you do to bring some sunshine to their lives?

Jane at ladies' day in TN:
West Fayetteville, 2003

Jane at ladies' retreat at Doublehead
Resort, Athens, AL, 1998

Jane at ladies' day,
St. Paul, MN, 1999

Remembering God

I saved the most important memory until last. I hope you have become more aware of the importance of memory—in the Scriptures, dealing with painful memories, discovering the treasures of our everyday lives, and making new memories. Remembering God is the most worthwhile of all the facets of the jewel called memory because it alone influences our eternal destiny.

Earliest Memories of God

As individuals we differ in our earliest memories of the Father. In preparation for this chapter, my mind drifted back to earlier days. Certain spiritual milestones seemed to stand out above all the other events. How well I remember the day of my baptism. I was not quite twelve years old when I responded to the invitation one night during a gospel meeting. The clothes I was wearing, even down to the color of my shoes and the silver buttons on my outfit, are just as vivid to me today as if the event had happened only yesterday. The following Sunday I made an entry in my diary about the meaningful experience of partaking of the Lord's supper.

Many times we see God in the eyes and hands of His servants who help us through the hurts of life.

Scenes of camp as a teenager will forever be etched in my memory—our devotionals by the lakeside when God seemed so close that I felt I could almost touch Him. The chapel singing at David Lipscomb University was always a highlight of my college days. During the early years of our service in the kingdom, our work with teenagers was a highlight. We took them on several mission meetings, camping out in natural surroundings. One place in particular was significant. After knocking doors and spending evenings in a gospel meeting, we concluded each day with a devotional. Our agreement was to cross a little bridge in silence to a campsite where we meditated on His Word and offered prayers and singing to our Father. God was very near and very real to all of us. We have joined hands with other Christians across the country in a number of endeavors—from small, rural churches to city auditoriums. God has always been there. So many times we could see Him in the eyes and in the hands of His servants who have helped us through the inevitable hurts of life. When we were involved in a head-on collision in 1970, God ministered to us in all our needs through fellow Christians. What priceless memories we have of those days!

Does God Move?

Because we are mere human beings, our emotions fluctuate in intensity. I cannot speak for others, but sometimes God seems very near to me and, at other times, He seems distant. During those distant times I always try to remind myself that I am the one who moves away, not God. He is right where I left Him. I am the one who drifts from time to time.

The success of any relationship depends on communication. Husbands and wives tend to drift apart when they do not honestly share their feelings. The same is true of parents and their children as well as friendships. We must keep the lines of communication open.

In the same respect, our relationship with God depends upon keeping the lines of communication open with Him. When the perfect law of liberty was completed, the Almighty no longer spoke directly to mankind. Instead, He now speaks to us through His written Word, and we speak to Him through prayer. The Bible and prayer! What meaningful avenues of communication between the divine and humans.

Remembering God's Word

During our dating days, Don and I were separated on weekdays for over a year. Between weekend dates, we kept the postal service in business with our daily letters. No one had to coax us into reading the letters the postman delivered because they were words from a loved one. How anxious we were to read their contents!

Dusty Words?

God has written some very meaningful words to us. How disappointed He must be when we allow dust to settle on them and view their reading as drudgery. Second Thessalonians 2:10 speaks of the deceitfulness of Satan and his success because "they did not receive the love of the truth, that they might be saved." Paul, in admonishing Timothy in 1 Timothy 4:13, exhorted the young man to "give attention to reading, to exhortation, to doctrine." In the second letter to Timothy this apostle urged him to "be diligent to present yourself approved to God, a worker who does not need to be ashamed, rightly dividing the word of truth" (2 Timothy 2:15). In Luke's account of the conversion of the Ethiopian eunuch, Phillip found the man reading the inspired words of Isaiah as he sat in his chariot on his journey home from Jerusalem. In Revelation 1:3 John pronounced a blessing on all those who read the Word of God.

Meditate on the Word

Meditation upon the Word is just as important as the reading. When Joshua assumed the leadership of the Israelites, God admonished him:

> This Book of the Law shall not depart from your mouth, but you shall meditate in it day and night, that you may observe to do according to all that is written in it. For then you will make your way prosperous, and then you will have good success (Joshua 1:8).

Later, in Psalm 19:14 David penned the following words: "Let the words of my mouth and the meditation of my heart be acceptable in Your sight, O Lord, my strength and my Redeemer." In another psalm David promised God: "My hands also I will lift up to Your commandments, which I love, and I will meditate on Your statutes" (Psalm 1119:48). Whenever I am working on a manuscript, some of my best thoughts come after I have planted the seed of the Word in my mind and have then gone about routine household tasks. I like to pull verses out of my subconscious mind as I cook, clean up the kitchen, fold the laundry, and do all the other daily demands of keeping a household functioning smoothly.

Time to Listen to God

Take time to let God talk to you. We are busy, too busy most of the time. Each day finds the urgent crowding out the important. Many women commute in heavy traffic to their jobs. When they leave that job, they again fight the traffic to begin their second shift, running necessary errands on the way home. Once there, they begin cooking supper while they wash several loads of clothes. After transporting their children to their various activities, overseeing their homework, and doing a little house-cleaning, they usually fall into bed exhausted. Their intentions were good, but they just couldn't seem to find a few minutes to let God talk to them through His Word.

Individuals vary in their internal clocks. Some people per-form their best mental work in the mornings and bomb out after supper. Others don't really come to life until the evening hours. Morning Bible study is out of the question for them! Realizing these differences, each of us should analyze our peak men-tal performance times and work with our own in-ternal timetables. If I may be permitted, as an older woman, I would like to pass on a little gem of wisdom to the younger ones. You will never get caught up with everything you need to do. There will always be some-thing screaming for your attention. If you wait until you have caught up to read God's Word, you will seldom get around to doing it. If you don't have time for a few minutes to read the Word, you are too busy! Prioritize and drop something. I have often told ladies in my classes that it is better to faithfully spend ten minutes a day in the Word than it is to designate longer periods of time and then fail to keep them. The best time may be when you first rise in the morning, or it may be dur-ing your lunch hour on the job, or waiting for your children at some activity, or before retiring. Pick your peak time, make a commitment, and then stick to it until it becomes a habit, a way of life, so you no longer have to think about doing it.

You will never get caught up with everything you need to do; something will always scream for your attention.

Tools for God's Time

Select needed tools. Just as a carpenter or a mechanic would not begin to do his work without some necessary tools, neither should we begin serious Bible study without some standard helps. Put them on your "hint" list for gift-giving occasions and you will soon have a good library.

- *A good Bible is necessary.* A Bible need not be expensive, but the print should be large enough to permit reading with ease. The King James, the New King James, the American Standard, and the New American Standard versions are the most reliable. Sometimes it is helpful to have other versions for comparative reading.

- *Bible dictionaries are useful.* For example, when we use the word *lamp*, a brass pole, a white shade, and a light bulb usually come to mind. When we read about lamps and lights in the Scriptures, we may need pictures to help us understand what their lamps were actually like in Bible days.

- *Concordances are essential.* Memory work has its place. It is nice to have some key passages and facts committed to memory. When I was a young girl, I was required to memorize the twelve sons of Jacob by one of my teachers, and I still remember their names. If you were to awaken me in the middle of the night now and ask me to recite those twelve tribes, I believe I could do it. Frankly, I don't know what practical use that particular memorization serves but it is locked inside my mind.

  As I have matured, I have found that familiarization, not memorization, of various verses is what is important. As long as I know one or two key words in that verse, it only requires a few minutes to locate the reference in a concordance. The more we read, the more familiar we become with the Word.

- *A good Bible geography book is most helpful.* Knowing where the various Bible accounts took place (and their proximity to other places) sheds much light on a study.

- *Commentaries are rich in their contents.* Remember that a commentary is only one person's opinion, but sometimes it is helpful to know what other people have learned through years of Bible study on a certain passage. The Gospel Advocate series, McGarvey's Commentaries, Clarke's Commentaries, Barnes' Notes, Coffman's Commentaries, as well as many others are useful.

- *Bible encyclopedias can shed much light.* The International Standard Bible Encyclopedia as well as McClintock and Strong Cyclopedia of Biblical Theological and Ecclesiastical Literature are two classics.

- *Church histories relate the story of the church through the ages.* The Eternal Kingdom by F. W. Mattox is one of the best histories.

- *Bible surveys condense a great deal of information into a small space.* There is a time when we need to pick verses apart as we try to understand every word. However, sometimes we can become so bogged down that we can't see the forest for the trees. How helpful it is to study a summary of each book of the Bible to make all the puzzle parts fit together. Once we get an overview of the forest, we can then go back and look at each tree.

> *Familiarization, not memorization, is what is important. It only requires a few minutes to locate it in a concordance.*

- *Greek studies throw additional light on the meanings of words.* The only way to unlock the true meanings of words is to consult some references books on the meanings of the originally inspired words. *The Analytical Greek Lexicon, The Interlinear Bible, Thayer Greek-English Lexicon of the New Testament, Vine's Expository Dictionary of Biblical Words,* and *Wuest's Word Studies* are some of my favorites. All of these are available for computer use.

Your Time with God

Making the Most of Your Time with God—a Place, a Plan

Designate a *place* for Bible study. We all tend to pursue activities that are most convenient. If we have to gather our materials each time we want to study, our time will be limited. Have a bookcase for your special books, a comfortable chair, and a desk.

Develop a *plan* for Bible study. Wars are not fought successfully without battle plans. Buildings will not last without sound architectural drawings. Neither will a Christian draw closer to God through His Word without some sort of plan for study. Individuals differ in what appeals to them. Through the years, the following suggestions have been some of my favorite methods to study. Perhaps you can find one that will fit your own personality. The important consideration to remember is to select a plan and stick with it.

1. *Begin your quiet time with a prayer for an open mind to God's words.*

2. *Read a chapter a day.* That is one method of study that is used by many.

3. *Select one of the Gospels and study a small portion each day.* Reading such books as *A Harmony of the Gospels* is a good way to compare the different Gospel accounts.

4. *Choose an epistle and duplicate the book from a large-print edition.* Paste one or two verses on each blank page in a loose-leaf notebook. As you use commentaries, concor-

dances, maps and other study helps, make notes on that page. When you have completed the epistle, you will find that you have written your own commentary that you will cherish all your life.

5. *Study by subjects, keeping your information in a small notebook.* For example, make a study of New Testament worship or the steps necessary for salvation. Write supporting verses in your notebook under each heading, along with historical data, and you will have a valuable tool for discussing the Bible with other people.

6. *Study a Bible-related subject such as evolution.* Purchase books on the subject.

7. *Study the geography of Palestine to deepen your understanding of the Bible.*

8. *Invest in workbooks on various subjects.* Most workbooks are intended for use in the classroom, but they also make excellent guides for personal home studies. Writing reinforces the learning process. When you have completed the workbook, you will have another valuable tool to be used in teaching others.

8. *Read surveys on the different books of the Bible.* Earlier in this study we discussed the importance of seeing the overall picture of a book of the Bible.

10. *Subscribe to several brotherhood periodicals.* It is wise to keep up with the doctrines that are being taught in the brotherhood. How foolish it is to bury our heads in the sand.

> *Workbooks make excellent guides for personal home studies. Writing reinforces the learning process.*

11. *Study with a friend.* If you have a neighbor or a friend at work who wants to learn more about the Bible, ask her to join you for a few minutes each day or even once a week. Not only will you learn more by sharing opinions, but this is also an excellent way to reach the lost. I know someone who has a weekly study in her home with some of her co-workers, as well as friends in her neighborhood. Many conversions have resulted.

12. *Listen to tapes of the Scriptures and related subjects.* This is an excellent way to better utilize the time spent dressing each morning, driving in the car, or cooking supper each night.

13. *Make a study of a favorite Bible character.* A number of years ago I wanted to learn more about the life of David because some of his words previously had a special meaning to me during a stressful time. I was teaching school at the time, so I spent some time each summer morning reading about the life of David and writing down my research. I divided his life into three major parts and studied one part each summer. During the winter months, I reviewed what I had written the previous summer. *Meet My Friend David* was the result of that study. A recent lectureship assignment called for an in-depth study of the life of Esther, which I thoroughly enjoyed. I would like for my next character study to be about Peter. I like him because I can identify with him; he was so human.

14. *Place verses in conspicuous areas—near your kitchen sink, on your bathroom mirror, at your desk at work, in your car.* As I mentioned earlier, I prefer verse familiarization rather than verse memorization. The important thing is to let God speak to you through that verse. If you read it twenty or thirty times a week, it will probably find a place in your heart.

15. *Use your waiting time wisely.* Whenever you have a doctor's appointment, take your study material with you. There's no need to fume and fuss because you have to wait. Relax and walk with the Master through His Word. Whenever Don has to spend some time in the hospital, I customarily pack a bag with my clothes. In addition, I also pack a small bag of study materials. Much of my published material was originally written by his bedside.

Your Prayers

God talks to His children through His Word and they, in turn, talk with Him through the avenue of prayer. What a blessed privilege it is to be permitted to enter into the presence of the Almighty with our petitions. Christians should pray at regular times, just as Daniel continued to pray at his accustomed time each day. That selected time depends upon the individual. In 1 Thessalonians 5:17 Christians are admonished to pray without ceasing. Naturally, we cannot pray twenty-four hours a day, but each day should be interspersed with continual prayers as we go about our routine tasks.

Each day should be interspersed with continual prayers as we go about our routine tasks.

The Model Prayer

In Matthew 6:9–13, after warning His followers about hypocritical prayers, Jesus gave them a model prayer. Christians should incorporate the various parts of this prayer in their own prayers throughout the day. I have found it useful to use little strips of colored felt over my kitchen sink to remind me of the different parts of the model prayer. The colors of the strips are yellow, green, blue, brown, red, black, and another yellow.

Pray for one section of your prayer when you get up in the mornings. Pray for another one on your lunch break. Make good use of the minutes involved in cooking and routine house-work, as well as in driving to work.

✠ **Praise** (yellow for royalty). "Our Father in heaven, Hallowed be Your name." All too often we plunge into our prayers with our requests of the Father without pausing to reflect upon His majesty. We should spend a few minutes praising God. It would be helpful to scan the book of Psalms for majestic phrases the writers used. We need to be aware of His sacred-ness and how privileged we are to enter His presence.

✠ **The Church** (green for growing). "Your kingdom come." Of course the kingdom (the church) now has come, but this would be a good time in our prayers to thank God for sending His son and for the establishment of the church. We can pause and pray for each elder and the other public servants by name, as well as the various programs of work. The church is being attacked from so many fronts today. We should pray for its purity as well as for our own ability to stand firm in the faith.

✠ **Submission to God's Will** (blue for the peace that comes from submission). "Your will be done on earth, as it is in heaven." Our lives should be lived in total submission to the Father's will.

✠ **Requests for Essentials** (brown to represent bread). "Give us this day our daily bread." Notice that Jesus did not teach His disciples to pray for food for next week or next month. He said daily bread. While we are asking God for essentials, it is a good time to thank Him for all the added luxuries He provides every day. (Be specific as you name them.)

- ***Forgiveness*** (red for indebtedness). "And forgive us our debts, as we forgive our debtors." When we ask for God's forgiveness, we should be specific about our sins instead of using blanket statements. "God, I goofed when I lost my patience in the traffic today. Please forgive me and help me remain calm tomorrow." "Father, the information I passed along to my friend was gossip. Forgive me for opening my mouth before I thought."

  We should always remember the sobering fact that we are forgiven as we forgive others who have wronged us. Before we ask for forgiveness for our own shortcomings, we should have a forgiving spirit toward those who have wronged us. In addition, we need to go to them and try to straighten out the dissention.

- ***Help in Overcoming*** *Our Weaknesses* (black for the bleakness of our weaknesses). "And lead us not into temptation, but deliver us from the evil one." This is an excellent time to ponder upon our weaknesses as we realize our own inadequacies and God's power. (Reflect on your weaknesses. You are not going to overcome them until you are first aware of them.)

- ***Praise*** (yellow to denote majesty). "For Yours is the kingdom and the power and the glory forever." Our prayers should begin and end with praise.

Intercession of Christ

At the time Christ taught His disciples how to pray, He had not yet ascended to heaven to act as our mediator (1 Timothy 2:5), but now He is there to intercede for us. When we make our requests, He can take them before God's throne and tell the Father that He knows how we feel because He once lived in a human body and faced similar temptations. What a blessing it is to have an advocate.

Petitions

Christ did not include our various petitions in His model prayer, but He taught the principle elsewhere. We should pray for the following people in addition to those in every other walk of life.

Sick	(James 5:13–15)
Lost	(Romans 10:1)
Civil Rulers	(1 Timothy 2:1–2)
Brethren	(Philippians 1:9–12)
Preachers	(1 Thessalonians 3:1–2)
Our Enemies	(Acts 7:60)

Prayer is powerful and should be used throughout the day.

Conclusion

The most important memories we can have in this life are the ones that center around our heavenly Father. For many years one of my favorite hymns has been "My God and I." Of course it cannot be sung literally because, since the perfect law of liberty has been completed, our Father speaks through His written Word instead of communing directly with human beings. A mature child of God realizes that the words are used in the sense of poetic license, but they portray our deep and meaningful relationship with God.

> My God and I go in the field together,
> We walk and talk as good friends should and do;
> We clasp our hands, our voices ring with laughter,
> My God and I walk thru the meadow's hue.
> My God and I will go for aye together,
> We'll walk and talk as good friends should and do;
> This earth will pass, and with it common trifles,
> But God and I will go unendingly.

We are offered a lifetime of walking and talking with our Father through prayer and the study of His Word. What precious memories they hold in store for us.

Questions for Thought

1. Share your most meaningful memories of your relationship with God and fellow Christians.

2. Why do we sometimes feel very close to God while at other times He seems far away? What is usually the problem?

3. What are our two lines of communication with God?

4. Discuss the following passages that deal with the importance of divine words: 1 Timothy 4:13; 2 Timothy 2:15; Acts 8:28–35; Revelation 1:3.

5. When Joshua assumed the leadership of the Israelites, what admonition did God give him? (Joshua 1:8).

6. What is the difference in merely reading scriptures and in meditating upon them?

7. Discuss how a person's internal clock affects her optimal study time.

8. The lesson listed some good tools to use in Bible study. Discuss which ones have been used by members of the class.

9. This chapter listed a number of different plans to help us focus on our Bible study. (You may want to add others.) Which ones appeal most to you?

10. God talks to us through His Word and we talk to Him through prayer. First Thessalonians 5:17 urges Christians to pray without ceasing. What does this mean?

11. Make a list of the elements given in the model prayer found in Matthew 6:9–13. Expand upon the suggestions given in the lesson.

12. What does the song *My God and I* mean to you?

Epilogue

Jane's Parting Words

I pray that this study has made a difference in your life, just as it has in mine. Why do I write? It is certainly not for fame or money. Although I cannot speak for other authors, I write because something very meaningful inside my heart simply must find expression.

Buried deeply within each of us is a necklace with beads of important events in our lives: birthdays, holiday celebrations, graduations, wedding ceremonies, new babies, new houses, new jobs. However, there are gold nuggets between each of these significant beads in our lives—daily living, the events we take for granted. But how priceless they are! I pray that you have learned to cherish their treasures.

This study has also dealt with painful memories. After studying the dynamics of memory, I hope we now better understand how our memories found a place in our hearts, as well as how to live with them. As I mentioned in *Let This Cup Pass*, some bridges must be burned behind us if we are to live useful, productive lives. However, it is most important to sift through their ashes for some other seldom-noticed nuggets of gold—the lessons we have learned from these hurtful experiences. They are priceless because they have the potential for molding us into caring, loving Christians who have a purpose in life much more important than any obstacles we may find in our pathways. As the wise rabbi concluded: "It's up to you, my friend. It's up to you."

My parting wish to each of you is to cultivate memories that will enable you to enjoy roses in the December phase of your life. Even more important, remember that we are all ultimately striving for that city where the roses never fade. May the familiar song that you have sung many times have new meaning in your life.

Where the Roses Never Fade

I am going to a city
Where the streets with gold are laid.
Where the tree of life is blooming,
And the roses never fade.
Here they bloom but for a season,
Soon their beauty is decayed;
I am going to a city
Where the roses never fade.